EXERCISES TO ACCOMPANY

English Simplified

Third Canadian Edition

Blanche Ellsworth

Arnold Keller
University of Victoria

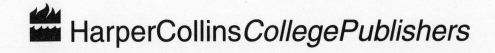

HarperCollins*CollegePublishers*

Acquisitions Editor: Brian Henderson
Project Coordination: Ruttle Graphics, Inc.
Text Design: Brand X Studio/Robin Hoffman
Cover Design: Molly Heron/Kay Petronio
Electronic Production Manager: Angel Gonzalez, Jr.
Manufacturing Manager: Willie Lane
Electronic Page Makeup: Ruttle Graphics, Inc.
Printer and Binder: Best Book Manufacturers
Cover Printer: Best Book Manufacturers

Exercises to Accompany English Simplified, Third Canadian Edition

ISBN: 0-673-999637

95 96 97 98 99 9 8 7 6 5 4 3 2 1

CONTENTS

PREFACE

The third Canadian edition of *Exercises to Accompany English Simplified* preserves the spirit and form of the first two editions. The exercises continue to offer practice in the comprehensive range of topics that is the hallmark of the *English Simplified* text. However, this latest volume also provides examples and sentences that reflect changing student populations and contemporary Canadian interests. Many exercises also ask students to respond more fully than in previous editions; this should help instructors identify what students know and what they don't. Other features include a brief glossary of terms and a convenient index to the *English Simplified* text; both should make it easier for students to find what they need.

A book like this has two main purposes: to help students become aware of language habits that may limit their performance and, by pinpointing errors, to help students correct them. No workbook can provide enough exercises to neutralize habitual errors; nor can a workbook itself ensure that students will transfer what they learn to their own essays. But a workbook can inform and guide students toward the practice and expectations of educated users of English.

An exercise that lets students guess at the right answer is unlikely to be effective. Throughout this workbook, therefore, we stress the need to know *why* a particular form is correct. Students typically must furnish not only the right answers but also the reasons for their choices. These techniques come from our own experiences in the classroom over more than four decades of teaching at San Francisco State University, Vanier College, and the University of Victoria. Indeed, we have drawn many of the sentences from student papers so as to represent the most frequently made errors.

Blanche Ellsworth
Arnold Keller

1. DIAGNOSTIC TEST: GRAMMAR

Sentences

In the blank after each item,

write **1** if the boldface expression is **one complete sentence;**
write **2** if it is a **fragment** (incorrect: less than a complete sentence);
write **3** if it is a **comma splice** or **fused sentence** (incorrect: two or more sentences written as one; also known as a **run-on**).

Example: Riel spent the year in jail. *Having refused to compromise his ideals.*   <u>2</u>

1. The choir had brought their music. *But no one asked them to sing.*   1. _____

2. The Prime Minister seemed happy to retire from politics. *His family looking forward to spending more time with him.*   2. _____

3. *In Russia, pork is sold for 465 rubles a pound* that amount is equivalent to the average monthly salary.   3. _____

4. The Leafs made two big trades after the season had begun. *First for a goalie and then for a centre.*   4. _____

5. The Caribbean Student Society put Martina Jones in charge of the Reggae Festival. *A responsibility that appealed to her.*   5. _____

6. *The weather improved about noon, we went for a walk on the beach.*   6. _____

7. Divorce is still prevalent in Canada. *About six out of every thousand people.*   7. _____

8. *Although the economy may seem worse, more people are volunteering to help the poor.*   8. _____

9. *The reason for her shyness being that she knew no one at the party except her hostess.*   9. _____

10. *The experiment to produce nuclear fusion was both controversial and exciting, scientists all over the world attempted to duplicate its results.*   10. _____

11. *Scientists have learned that bison can infect domestic livestock with a serious bacterial disease.*   11. _____

12. She loved all styles of art. *She said she particularly loved the impressionists, she had studied them in Paris.*   12. _____

13. We walked over to the lost-and-found office. *To see whether the bag had been turned in.*   13. _____

14. *The shift lever must be in neutral only then will the car start.*   14. _____

15. *They were driven back by the flames, they could find no way out.* The end seemed near.   15. _____

16. *If you want an unusual form of exercise, learn to play the bagpipes.*   16. _____

Grammar

In the blank after each sentence,

write **1** if the boldface expression is used **correctly**;
write **0** if it is used **incorrectly**.

Example: There *is* just three shopping days before Christmas.   0

1. The professor assured Mark and *I* that we could still pass the course.   1. _____

2. Bill was fired from his new job, *which* made him despondent.   2. _____

3. Each member will be responsible for *their* own transportation.   3. _____

4. There *was* at least two windows in each room.   4. _____

5. Several of *us* newcomers needed a map to find our way around.   5. _____

6. Every filing clerk and typist *was* asked to attend an afternoon meeting.   6. _____

7. The professor and *myself* met for a review session.   7. _____

8. Surprisingly enough, Joan Smith was leading *not only* in the suburbs *but also* in the rural areas.   8. _____

9. In each packet *were* a program guide, a notepad, and a pen.   9. _____

10. Leave the message with *whoever* answers the phone.   10. _____

11. *Having made no other plans for the evening,* Tony was glad to accept the invitation.   11. _____

12. Everyone in the Aboriginal Society *was* urged to join the movement to bring more Native Canadian faculty to campus.   12. _____

13. If I *was* queen, you'd be my king.   13. _____

14. I bought one of the printers that *were* on sale.   14. _____

15. There *were* five different Asian student organizations on campus.   15. _____

16. *Do* either of you have an estimate for the repairs?   16. _____

17. The director, as well as the choir members, *has* agreed to appear on television.   17. _____

18. The supervisor is especially fond of arranging training programs, working on elaborate projects, and *to develop budgets.*   18. _____

19. Zack, *hoping to impress Tomiko with his knowledge of Japanese cooking,* prepared an elaborate meal.   19. _____

20. *Who* do you think mailed the anonymous letter to the editor?   20. _____

21. Neither the students nor the instructor *knows* where the notice is to be posted.   21. _____

22. Are you sure that it was *him* that you saw last evening?   22. _____

23. Between you and *me,* her account of the robbery sounded rather strange.   23. _____

24. *Hoping to find part-time employment,* Sheila made an appointment at the campus placement office.   24. _____

25. He joined the Big Brothers Organization and coached in minor hockey. *It* was expected of him.   25. _____

26. Given the candidates, it's painfully clear that *us* voters didn't have much of a choice.   26. _____

27. Tom prepared the meal *like* the directions indicated.   27. _____

28. Tension *is when* one experiences nervous strain and anxiety.   28. _____

29. *While carrying my books to the library,* a squirrel darted across my path.   29. _____

2

30. Norma *only* had one issue left to raise before she could rest her case.   30. _____

31. I had no idea that *my* giving a report would create such turmoil at the meeting.   31. _____

32. We didn't think that many of *us* substitutes would get into the game.   32. _____

33. Dean Robert Patterson gave Karen and *I* permission to establish a volunteer organization to tutor inner-city students.   33. _____

34. Although he often spoke harshly to others, his voice sounded *pleasant* to us.   34. _____

35. Neither the librarian nor the students in the reference room *was* aware of the situation.   35. _____

36. Professor Rogers looks very *differently* since he shaved his beard.   36. _____

37. There is no question that it was *she* behind the curtain.   37. _____

38. Bob had always been more curious about the family's Irish ancestors than *he.*   38. _____

39. Dr. Smith, together with thirty of his students, *are* going on a field trip.   39. _____

40. Each of the employees *were* given an opportunity to offer a solution to the problem.   40. _____

41. *Eiko Bailey's* taking a part-time position meant that she had to budget her time carefully.   41. _____

42. *Standing motionless on that windswept, dreary plain,* the rain pelted my face.   42. _____

43. I had agreed to *promptly and without delay* notify them of my decision.   43. _____

44. The dean agreed to award the scholarship to *whomever* the committee selected.   44. _____

45. *Knowing that I should study,* it seemed wise for me not to go to the game.   45. _____

46. *Who* were you trying to find in the auditorium yesterday?   46. _____

47. The noise and the general chaos caused by the alarm *were* disturbing to the visitor.   47. _____

48. As hard as I try, I doubt if I'll ever make as much money as *her.*   48. _____

49. Only one of these stamps *is* of real value.   49. _____

50. The guide showed Carol and *myself* all the main points of interest.   50. _____

2. DIAGNOSTIC TEST: PUNCTUATION

In the blank after each sentence,

write **1** if the punctuation in brackets is **correct;**
write **0** if it is **incorrect.**

(Use only one number in each blank.)

Example: Mr[.] Eliot worked in a bank.   1

Example: Regular exercise and sound nutritional habits[,] are essential for good health.   0

1. Modern writers are often directly and profoundly influenced by the past[;] in fact, we can't fully study their work without knowing the traditions they draw on.   1. _____

2. A good horror movie doesn't merely scare us[,] it shows us worlds we never imagined.   2. _____

3. "Why can't a woman be more like a man["?] the chauvinist asked.   3. _____

4. I learned that the newly elected officers were Susie Wong, president[;] Denzell Jones, vice-president[;] Sandra Smith, treasurer[;] and Marie LeClerc, secretary.   4. _____

5. The class expected low grades[. T]he test having been long and difficult.   5. _____

6. It[']s hard to imagine life without a VCR, a personal computer, and a microwave oven.   6. _____

7. Eventually, everybody comes to Rick's[;] the best saloon in Casablanca.   7. _____

8. Recognizing that unemployment places stress on younger people[,] the provincial officials are restructuring its job training program for the post secondary educational system.   8. _____

9. Richard Chen was unhappy at his college[,] he missed hearing Chinese and enjoying his favourite foods.   9. _____

10. That is not the Sullivans' boat; at least, I think that it isn't their[']s.   10. _____

11. After penicillin was first mass-produced[,] infant mortality decreased significantly.   11. _____

12. Inspector Trace asked, "Is that all you remember?["""]Are you sure?"   12. _____

13. "The report is ready," Chisholm said[,] "I'm sending it to the supervisor today."   13. _____

14. Didn't I hear you say, "I especially like blueberry pie"[?]   14. _____

15. Joe enrolled in a community college[;] although he had planned originally to attend a university. 15. _____

16. Stanley moved to Windsor[,] where he hoped to open a restaurant.   16. _____

17. That was a bit too close for comfort[,] wasn't it?   17. _____

18. The advertiser received more than two[-]hundred replies.   18. _____

19. Sarah is asking for two week[']s vacation to visit relatives in the Arctic.   19. _____

20. On February 21, 1995[,] Robin and Sam are getting married.   20. _____

21. The womens['] basketball team has reached the quarter finals.   21. _____

22. Many urban areas face major social problems[;] such as unemployment, drug rings, and racial and ethnic tension.   22. _____

23. She received twenty[-]three greeting cards on her sixtieth birthday.   23. _____

24. He hurried across the campus[,] and up the steps of the library.   24. _____

25. Many weeks before school was out[;] he had applied for a summer job.   25. _____

26. Dear Sir[;] Can you use an extra cashier in your store this summer?   26. _____

27. Schweitzer summed up his ethics as "reverence for life[,]" a phrase that came to him during his early years in Africa.   27. _____

28. Our communications professor asked us if we understood the use of extended periods of silence often found in conversations among Inuit people[?]   28. _____

29. "As for who won the election[—]well, not all the votes have been counted," she said.   29. _____

30. Polly asked ["]if I had seen where she had put her glasses.[']   30. _____

31. Any music[,] that is not jazz[,] does not appeal to him.   31. _____

32. "Election results are coming in quickly now," the newscaster announced[;] "and we should be able to declare the winner soon."   32. _____

33. The gates are locked[,] therefore, we shall have to visit the museum some other day.   33. _____

34. The children went to the zoo[;] bought ice-cream cones[;] fed peanuts to the elephants[;] and watched the seals perform their tricks while being fed.   34. _____

35. The camp director said, "The children like to sing ["]For He's a Jolly Good Fellow.["]   35. _____

36. Midori Ito, who is noted for her superb jumping skills, did not do well in the 1992 Olympics[;] but Karen Preston, who is praised for her artistic style, landed her jumps during the final competition.   36. _____

37. "Sesame Street" is produced by the Childrens['] Television Workshop.   37. _____

38. Late-night television viewers should be cautious when watching a home-shopping network[,] because they may purchase items that they don't need.   38. _____

39. Because he had watched a late show on television[,] he failed to hear his alarm clock.   39. _____

40. Because of minimal academic standards[,] many high school students don't study much.   40. _____

41. That distinguished gentleman wearing the gray suit[,] has represented us in the legislature for twenty years.   41. _____

42. The scholarship award went to Anna Brown, the student[,] who had the highest grades.   42. _____

43. Some of the technologies developed after World War II were[:] television, synthetic fibers, and air travel.   43. _____

44. Samantha soon found that all the foods[,] which she especially liked[,] were high in calories.   44. _____

45. Esther Greenberg[,] who is my roommate[,] comes from a small town.   45. _____

46. "Only two people hav[']ent completed the assignment," the teacher said.   46. _____

47. The talk show host[,] irritated and impatient[,] cut off the caller who insisted he was calling from aboard a flying saucer.   47. _____

48. She went grocery shopping[,] her salary check having arrived in the afternoon mail.   48. _____

49. A note under the door read: "Sorry you weren't in. The Emerson[']s."   49. _____

50. The Canadian population is changing dramatically[,] Asian and East Indian immigration has increased significantly.   50. _____

51. He chopped wood for the fireplace[;] he piled the logs on the hearth.   51. _____

52. The movie did not sell many tickets[.] Because nobody wanted to watch a four-hour documentary about dry cleaning.   52. _____

53. The two boys, not knowing their way in the city[;] asked for directions.   53. _____

5

54. By saving her money[,] Laura was able to attend university.   54. _____

55. To gain recognition as a speaker[;] he accepted all invitations to appear before civic groups.   55. _____

56. Sue Allen[,] who is a second–year student [,] is the chairperson of the Student Appeals Committee.   56. _____

57. Any candidate[,] who wants to increase social programs[,] will probably be defeated during
    elections held in the 1990s.   57. _____

58. "Oh dear[,] I hope I'm not late," said Joyce.   58. _____

59. "I cannot believe that you have not read my book!"[,] shouted the author to the critic.   59. _____

60. While speaking, the club president never knew the moment[,] at which someone might interrupt
    him.   60. _____

61. We considered going to a movie[,] when our classes were over.   61. _____

62. The city hall having burned to the ground[,] the townspeople undertook plans to replace it.   62. _____

63. My hometown is a place[,] where men still think white shoes and belts are high fashion.   63. _____

64. She spent her student teaching practicum in Courtney[,] where she also went to hockey games
    regularly.   64. _____

65. Having learned that she was eligible for a scholarship[,] she turned in her application.   65. _____

66. The fact that he had not yet found a place to live[,] did not especially bother him.   66. _____

67. Stand with your hips flush against the wall[,] then see how far forward you can bend without losing
    your balance.   67. _____

68. Many Canadians remember rituals and celebrations from their childhood[,] moreover, they are
    seeking ways to incorporate some of these rituals into their busy lives.   68. _____

69. Polio survivors are reaching their forties and fifties[;] they are discovering new medical problems
    associated with their bouts with polio.   69. _____

70. Because many university students are vegetarians[;] many campus dining rooms now offer a
    vegetarian meal plan.   70. _____

71. The real estate agent[,] who sold our house[,] offered many tips on how to prepare our house for
    the market.   71. _____

72. To save money[,] purchase personalized checks through a company other than your bank.   72. _____

73. The parking lot always is full[,] when there is a soccer game on campus.   73. _____

74. Hoping for a better understanding of another culture[:] our family decided to host an international
    exchange student for the spring semester.   74. _____

75. The student promised to finish the paper[,] and turn it in by the end of the day.   75. _____

3. DIAGNOSTIC TEST: MECHANICS, SPELLING, USAGE

Capitalization

In each blank,

> write **1** if the boldface word(s) **follow** the rules of capitalization;
> write **0** if they do not.

Example: Margaret Laurence was born in
Neepawa. ___1___

Example: She comes from my **City.** ___0___

1. All **Students** must attend. 1. _____

2. My **college** days were stressful. 2. _____

3. He attends Mt. Douglas **high school.** 3. _____

4. The **Premier** changed his mind. 4. _____

5. Harry decided to go to school in the
East. 5. _____

6. She sent her **Mother** a gift. 6. _____

7. I failed **french** again. 7. _____

8. She is in France; **He** is at home. 8. _____

9. "Are you working?" **she** asked. 9. _____

10. I love **Chinese** food. 10. _____

11. We saluted the **canadian** flag. 11. _____

12. Last **Summer** I worked in a store. 12. _____

13. My birthday was on **Friday.** 13. _____

14. I am enrolled in courses in
philosophy and Japanese. 14. _____

15. She went **north** for Christmas. 15. _____

16. Please, **Father,** send me $500. 16. _____

17. My **Aunt Lisa** came to visit. 17. _____

18. "Stop!" **shouted** the officer. 18. _____

19. Jane refused to be **Chair** of the
committee. 19. _____

20. "If possible," he said, "**Write** the report
today." 20. _____

Abbreviations and Numbers

In each blank,

> write **1** if the boldface abbreviation or number is used **correctly;**
> write **0** if it is used **incorrectly.**

Example: I love **NY.** ___0___

1. **Six million** people died. 1. _____

2. He is now **21** years old. 2. _____

3. The show starts at **8** A.M. 3. _____

4. Dana was born on May **1st,** 1970. 4. _____

5. The rent is **$325** a month. 5. _____

6. The interest comes to **8** percent. 6. _____

7. I need to talk to the **prof.** 7. _____

8. There are **nineteen** women in the club. 8. _____

9. **1993** was another bad year for farmers. 9. _____

10. I wrote a note to **Dr.** Levy. 10. _____

11. He works at the Swiss Import **Co.** 11. _____

12. She lives on Chartwell **Ave.** 12. _____

13. We consulted Richard Gold, **Ph.D.** 13. _____

14. Our appointment is at **4** o'clock. 14. _____

15. I slept only **3** hours last night. 15. _____

Spelling

In each sentence, **one** boldface word is **misspelled**; write its number in the blank.

Example: (1) *Its* (2) *too* late (3) *to* go.	1

1. Jane's (1) *independent* attitude sometimes was a (2) *hindrence* to the (3) *committee.*   1. _____

2. (1) *Approximatly* half of the class noticed the (2) *omission* of the last item on the (3) *questionnaire.*   2. _____

3. The (1) *mischievous* child was (2) *persistant* about behaving in a (3) *ridiculous* manner.   3. _____

4. At the office, Jack was described as a (1) *conscientous,* (2) *courteous,* and (3) *indispensable* staff member.   4. _____

5. Even though Dave was (1) *competant* in his (2) *mathematics* class, he didn't have the (3) *discipline* required to work through the daily homework.   5. _____

6. The researcher's (1) *analysis* of the (2) *apparent* (3) *prejudise* that existed among the subjects in the experiment prompted him to write several essays as well as a journal article.   6. _____

7. She was (1) *particularly* (2) *sensable* about maintaining a study (3) *schedule.*   7. _____

8. It was (1) *necesary* to curb Jane's (2) *tendency* to interrupt the staff discussion with (3) *irrelevant* comments.   8. _____

9. (1) *Personaly,* it was no (2) *surprise* to me that the little boy's (3) *curiosity* prompted him to smear lipstick on the bathroom walls.   9. _____

10. Within just a few days, Al developed a (1) *procedure* on the computer for creating our (2) *bussiness* (3) *calendar.*   10. _____

11. As a (1) *sophomore,* Mary displayed the (2) *perseverence* and (3) *sacrifice* required to work three part-time jobs and to take five courses.   11. _____

12. Her (1) *opinion,* while (2) *fascinating,* revealed an indisputable (3) *hypocricy.*   12. _____

13. Every day our (1) *secretery* meets her friend from the (2) *Psychology* Department at their favourite campus (3) *restaurant.*   13. _____

14. During (2) *adolescence,* we often (2) *condemm* anyone who offers (3) *guidance.*   14. _____

15. Based on Bill's (1) *description,* his dream vacation sounded (2) *irresistable* and guaranteed to (3) *fulfill* anyone's need to escape.   15. _____

Usage

In the blank after each sentence,

write **1** if the boldface expression is used **correctly;**
write **0** if it is used **incorrectly.**

Example: St. John's is the provincial **capitol.**   0

1. Her report is different *than* mine.   1. _____

2. I'm not nervous; I'm *alright.*   2. _____

3. The plane began its *descent* for Regina.   3. _____

4. A slowdown in construction always *impacts* our business.   4. _____

5. My glasses *lay* where I had put them.   5. _____

6. I *seldom ever* go walking in the morning.   6. _____

7. We didn't play *good* in the last quarter.   7. _____

8

8. I decided to buy a *nice* birthday card. 8. _____

9. The clock was *lying* on its side. 9. _____

10. No one predicted the *affects* of the bomb. 10. _____

11. My aunt always uses unusual *stationery.* 11. _____

12. I dislike *those kind* of people. 12. _____

13. We are going to *canvas* the faculty for the scholarship fund. 13. _____

14. The computer *sits* on a small table. 14. _____

15. The *woman fire fighter* was hired last summer. 15. _____

16. The *principal* spoke to the students. 16. _____

17. I *had ought* to learn to use that software. 17. _____

18. *On the basis of* the report, the committee voted against the proposal. 18. _____

19. *Almost* everyone had left. 19. _____

20. He made *less* mistakes than I did. 20. _____

21. The family *better* check the smoke detectors in the house. 21. _____

22. The package had *burst* open. 22. _____

23. Ms. Grundy *censured* so much of the play, it was unintelligible. 23. _____

24. Children are being taught to consider the feelings of their *fellow man.* 24. _____

25. *Irregardless* of the dense fog, I drove. 25. _____

26. Four provinces *comprise* Western Canada. 26. _____

27. The beige walls *complement* the living room furniture. 27. _____

28. The student had *less* sources than were required for the research paper. 28. _____

29. I phoned *in regard to* employment. 29. _____

30. I *ought to of* called you. 30. _____

4. GRAMMAR: PARTS OF A SENTENCE

(Study Sections 1–3, The Sentence and Its Parts.)

One of the numbers beneath each sentence marks the point where the **complete subject** ends and the **complete predicate** begins. Write that number in the blank.

Example: Recently ₁ Europe ₂ has suffered several ₃ severe weather disasters.   2

1. The Statue of Liberty ₁ was restored ₂ and reopened ₃ in 1988.   1. _____

2. Many of the abandoned railroad stations ₁ of Canada and the United States ₂ have been restored ₃ for other uses.   2. _____

3. Artist Henri ₁ Matisse, who lived to be eighty-four years old, ₂ left a legacy of paintings, paper cutouts, sculptures, drawings, ₃ and prints.   3. _____

4. The editor ₁ wrote a kind note ₂ after the long list of changes ₃ to be made before final printing.   4. _____

5. Word processors, ₁ with their power to make editing easy, ₂ allow writers to revise ₃ as often as they wish.   5. _____

6. I ₁ recently completed ₂ a twenty-page research paper ₃ on the proposed common currency for all European countries.   6. _____

7. Which ₁ of the three word processing software packages ₂ has ₃ the best thesaurus?   7. _____

8. Rarely would she leave her apartment after his death. [*This inverted-word-order sentence, rewritten in subject-predicate order, becomes* She ₁ would rarely ₂ leave ₃ her apartment after his death.]   8. _____

9. Which ₁ of the polls ₂ examined the opinions ₃ of underrepresented populations from rural areas of the country?   9. _____

10. When did the dean and the director of admissions decide on your acceptance? [*Rewritten in subject-predicate order:* The dean ₁ and the director ₂ of admissions ₃ did ₄ decide ₅ on your acceptance when?]   10. _____

Write **1** if the boldface word is a **subject** (or part of a compound subject).
Write **2** if it is a **predicate** (verb).
Write **3** if it is a **complement** (or part of a compound complement).
(Use the first column for the first boldface word, the second column for the second.)

Example: *Wendell* played a great *game.*   1 3

Example: The *crew* of the ship *was* afraid.   1 2

1. *All* perform their tragic *play.*   1. ___ ___

2. Champion athletes *spend* much *time* training and competing.   2. ___ ___

3. *Time* and *tide* wait for no one.   3. ___ ___

4. Many *athletes worry* about life after the pros.   4. ___ ___

5. The populist *theme* in Western Canada from the last election *may survive* until the next election.   5. ___ ___

6. The *Committee voted* unanimously against the appointment.   6. ___ ___

7. The clustered *lights* far below the plane were *cities.*   7. ___ ___

8. A beacon *lights* the *runway* for arriving planes at night.   8. ___ ___

9. Often the consequences of failure in a career are personal *depression* and economic *hardship.*   9. ___ ___

10. *We peeked* at the latest draft of Sam's romance novel.   10. ___ ___

5. GRAMMAR: PARTS OF SPEECH

(Study Sections 4–9, The Parts of Speech: A Survey.)
Write the number (**1** to **8**, from the list below) of the **part of speech** of each boldface word.

1. noun	3. verb	5. adverb	7. conjunction
2. pronoun	4. adjective	6. preposition	8. interjection

Example: Munro writes **stories.**   __1__

1. Molly is a **singer** in a band.   1. _____
2. You must **replace** the alternator.   2. _____
3. **She** anticipated the vote.   3. _____
4. The new law affected **all.**   4. _____
5. Robert felt **tired.**   5. _____
6. She was **here** a moment ago.   6. _____
7. The **primary** goal is to reduce spending. 7. _____
8. The test was hard **but** fair.   8. _____
9. Do you want fries **with** that?   9. _____
10. **This** book is mine.   10. _____
11. **This** is the car to buy.   11. _____
12. She lives **across** the street.   12. _____
13. Is this **your** book?   13. _____
14. The book is **mine.**   14. _____
15. He wants an **education.**   15. _____
16. **Oh dear,** the professor looks confused. 16. _____
17. He agreed to proceed **slowly.**   17. _____
18. They **were sleeping** soundly at noon.   18. _____
19. The candidate took an **unpopular** position.   19. _____
20. She is **unusually** talented.   20. _____
21. **Everyone** joined in the protest.   21. _____
22. The **synagogue** is a landmark.   22. _____
23. Students from all parts of the city **had come** to the rally.   23. _____
24. The workers took a **strike** vote.   24. _____
25. He is the one **whom** I suspect.   25. _____

26. The researcher plays a video game **while** waiting for the results.   26. _____
27. What is your **plan?**   27. _____
28. Nancy **is** a strong feminist.   28. _____
29. No one came **after** ten o'clock.   29. _____
30. Put the book **there.**   30. _____
31. I saw him **once.**   31. _____
32. The **theatre** was dark.   32. _____
33. The band owns a **factory.**   33. _____
34. Weren't **you** surprised?   34. _____
35. They waited **for** us.   35. _____
36. The oil spill was very **damaging.**   36. _____
37. Did you pay your **dues?**   37. _____
38. **All** survivors were calm.   38. _____
39. **All** were calm.   39. _____
40. The student read **quickly.**   40. _____
41. She **became** an executive.   41. _____
42. **Well,** what shall we do now?   42. _____
43. He worked **during** the summer.   43. _____
44. **Tomorrow** is her birthday.   44. _____
45. Will she call **tomorrow?**   45. _____
46. **If** I go, will you come?   46. _____
47. The executive stood **behind** her staff.   47. _____
48. He **should** never **have been advanced** in rank.   48. _____
49. The party seemed **wild.**   49. _____
50. Iris arrived at the park **early.**   50. _____

6. GRAMMAR: PARTS OF SPEECH

(Study 4–9, The Parts of Speech: A Survey.)

Write the number (**1** to **8,** from the list below) of the **part of speech** of each boldface word:
  1. **noun**   3. **verb**   5. **adverb**   7. **conjunction**
  2. **pronoun**   4. **adjective** 6. **preposition** 8. **interjection**

Example: Judy planned to become a
            surgeon.   1
                                                               _____

  1. ***Clarify*** what you mean.   1. _____
  2. The letter should arrive ***today.***   2. _____
  3. ***What*** is the theme of the poem?   3. _____
  4. She ***never*** confides in anyone.   4. _____
  5. ***May*** I ***call*** you early on Friday?   5. _____
  6. ***Scary*** monsters crept into the little boy's
     dreams.   6. _____
  7. The weather was grey ***and*** miserable.   7. _____
  8. They ***are*** business associates.   8. _____
  9. ***Which*** is your locker?   9. _____
 10. Write to me ***when*** you can.   10. _____
 11. ***He*** cannot believe her reply.   11. _____
 12. ***Neither*** of the candidates spoke.   12. _____
 13. ***The*** journey proved quite hazardous.   13. _____
 14. The ***house*** was quiet.   14. _____
 15. With a few more votes, Hansen
     would have been elected.   15. _____
 16. ***Ah,*** I thought you would agree.   16. _____
 17. She spoke with genuine ***feeling.***   17. _____
 18. Mr. Wilson ***is*** a registered pharmacist. 18. _____
 19. The jury decided that there was
     criminal intent.   19. _____
 20. The students ***are calculating*** their
     grade point averages.   20. _____
 21. ***Maple*** trees in Quebec are threatened
     by acid rain.   21. _____
 22. He objected ***strenuously.***   22. _____

 23. This plane goes ***to*** Vancouver.   23. _____
 24. He is a real ***diplomat.***   24. _____
 25. ***Unless*** you qualify, you will be unable
     to compete.   25. _____
 26. Emily stood ***motionless.***   26. _____
 27. Emily seemed in perpetual ***motion.***   27. _____
 28. Give the report to either Becca ***or***
     Emily.   28. _____
 29. This fall, the new television shows
     were predictable ***and*** disappointing.   29. _____
 30. Do you recognize ***this*** name?   30. _____
 31. ***Somebody*** will surely notify you.   31. _____
 32. She lives ***on*** a ranch in Alberta.   32. _____
 33. The motive for the crime will ***soon***
     become clear.   33. _____
 34. ***This*** is a thankless task.   34. _____
 35. ***Accept*** the offer without delay.   35. _____
 36. I arrived ***too*** late to see him.   36. _____
 37. Everybody talks ***about*** the weather.   37. _____
 38. The MP spoke ***cautiously*** on the
     topic of illegal immigrants.   38. _____
 39. You are ***now*** approaching Paris.   39. _____
 40. The car was not new, but ***it*** was in
     good condition.   40. _____
 41. ***Roth*** never published a second novel.   41. _____
 42. He ***has*** always ***liked*** good food.   42. _____
 43. We plan to make ***an*** early start.   43. _____
 44. I want an ***up-to-date*** directory.   44. _____
 45. The animosity ***between*** the
     representatives was ardent.   45. _____

46. The country **should have established** better trade agreements with the major industrial powers.

46. _____

47. He fell **because** he was dizzy.

47. _____

48. **None** of the students failed.

48. _____

49. Gould began to play **beautifully.**

49. _____

50. Supplies were **not** available.

50. _____

7. GRAMMAR: PARTS OF SPEECH AND THEIR USES

(Study 4–9, The Parts of Speech: A Survey.)
In the first column, write the number (**1** to **8,** from the list below) of the **part of speech** of each boldface word. In the second column, write the number (**9** to **25,** from the list) that tells how the word is used: note that the terms in the second column are bundled together with brackets.

1. noun	**9. subject**
2. pronoun	**10. direct object**
	11. indirect object
	12. subjective complement
	13. objective complement
	14. object of preposition
3. verb	**15. predicate**
4. adjective	**16. modifying noun or pronoun**
	17. subjective complement
	18. objective complement
5. adverb	**19. modifying verb**
	20. modifying adjective
	21. modifying adverb
6. preposition	**22. introducing prepositional phrase**
7. conjunction	**23. coordinating: joining words, phrases, or clauses of equal rank**
	24. subordinating: introducing dependent clause
8. interjection	**25. showing emotion**

	Part of Speech	Use		Part of Speech	Use
Example: The *Canucks* were defeated.	1	9	13. He does *well* on tests.	13. ___	___
1. You *expect* me to believe that?	1. ___	___	14. She spoke *very* slowly.	14. ___	___
2. She is a soccer *star.*	2. ___	___	15. The *repetition* gets boring after awhile.	15. ___	___
3. *What!* It can't be true!	3. ___	___	16. Lunch was just *soup.*	16. ___	___
4. A *spreading* pessimism hit the stock market.	4. ___	___	17. He drives *carefully.*	17. ___	___
5. Donate *them* to the needy.	5. ___	___	18. He took her *advice.*	18. ___	___
6. He seems *unfriendly.*	6. ___	___	19. Many women cry *at* the monument.	19. ___	___
7. No one came with *me.*	7. ___	___	20. Up the aisle came *Joan* with a large shopping cart.	20. ___	___
8. Aren't *these* your keys?	8. ___	___	21. We rented *a* car.	21. ___	___
9. The newspaper looks more *like* a magazine.	9. ___	___	22. The city was troubled *but* hopeful about rebuilding.	22. ___	___
10. *Whom* did your friend see?	10. ___	___	23. The path was *muddy.*	23. ___	___
11. The movie surprised most *critics.*	11. ___	___	24. He looked *good* in his new professional attire.	24. ___	___
12. *Oh,* so that's it!	12. ___	___			

		Part of Speech	Use

25. I was *too* surprised to answer. 25. _____ _____

26. Repeat the first *step.* 26. _____ _____

27. *Who* is afraid of them? 27. _____ _____

28. Isn't *this* the last street? 28. _____ _____

29. He played *very* well. 29. _____ _____

30. *Since* he was late for class, he ran. 30. _____ _____

31. *Look* at the flags! 31. _____ _____

32. The premier gave *Thompson* an order. 32. _____ _____

33. She ran *quickly.* 33. _____ _____

34. "*Hurrah!*" we yelled. 34. _____ _____

35. The relief efforts after the storm seemed incredibly *slow.* 35. _____ _____

36. *Has* he *called* yet? 36. _____ _____

37. The Canadian cultural mosaic is *complex.* 37. _____ _____

38. *Biology* is her major. 38. _____ _____

39. My son gave his *friend* a poster. 39. _____ _____

		Part of Speech	Use

40. *Everyone* went to the rally except me. 40. _____ _____

41. He seems *truly* sorry. 41. _____ _____

42. *Yes,* many students are tutoring children. 42. _____ _____

43. It was a *silly* remark. 43. _____ _____

44. The television documentary addressed questions *about* Quebec separatism. 44. _____ _____

45. *Which* will be selected? 45. _____ _____

46. Will you tell him, *or* shall I? 46. _____ _____

47. The computer analyst considered the program *complete.* 47. _____ _____

48. His chances seemed *good.* 48. _____ _____

49. Listening *and* surveillance devices are part of the standard equipment. 49. _____ _____

50. The corporate interview was *brutal.* 50. _____ _____

8. GRAMMAR: COMPLEMENTS

(Study Section 11B, Complement.)

Write the number that tells how the boldface complement is used:

1. **direct object**   3. **subjective complement**
2. **indirect object**   4. **objective complement**

Example: Alex and Mallory took the *car.* ___1___

1. He has been an *environmentalist* for thirty years. 1. _____

2. This dessert is too *sweet.* 2. _____

3. We gave the *car* a shove. 3. _____

4. He is writing his *memoirs.* 4. _____

5. The logging industry has lost *jobs* to international competitors. 5. _____

6. How can something taste *"light"?* 6. _____

7. Is he to be a *candidate?* 7. _____

8. Please give *me* your address. 8. _____

9. Canada made Ottawa its *capital.* 9. _____

10. She lent me a *map* of Windsor. 10. _____

11. Give *me* your solemn promise. 11. _____

12. The student conducted an *experiment.* 12. _____

13. She sounds *happier* every day. 13. _____

14. The mechanic actually reduced the *bill.* 14. _____

15. The university offered *her* an opportunity to do research. 15. _____

16. John installed another *hard drive* in his computer. 16. _____

17. She is a talented *actress.* 17. _____

18. Harry is the *judge* for the talent show this year. 18. _____

19. Pam won a *scholarship.* 19. _____

20. Have you sent *copies* of the minutes to the members? 20. _____

21. *Whom* did you meet yesterday? 21. _____

22. Who designed the *plaque?* 22. _____

23. She is a *finalist* now. 23. _____

24. Will the professor give *John* another chance? 24. _____

25. The sun on Malcolm's back felt *good.* 25. _____

26. Politicians will promise *us* anything. 26. _____

27. She gave me no *chance* to object. 27. _____

28. She is writing an *editorial.* 28. _____

29. The group has been studying *anthropology* for three semesters. 29. _____

30. She has been earning *money* ever since she was eleven years old. 30. _____

31. Either she or I will call *you.* 31. _____

32. Her former employer gave *her* the idea for the small business. 32. _____

33. His proposal sounded *foolish.* 33. _____

34. *Which* did the professor choose? 34. _____

35. I named him my *beneficiary.* 35. _____

36. Who were the city *champions* last year? 36. _____

37. She is an *instructor* at the community college. 37. _____

38. She gave *me* no clue regarding her identity. 38. _____

39. That will be *all,* Hudson. 39. _____

40. I made an *appointment* with my new adviser. 40. _____

41. She became an *administrator.* 41. _____

42. I agreed to consider his *offer.* 42. _____

43. He considered her a *genius.* 43. _____

44. Select whatever *medium* you like for your art project.

44. _____

45. The company made her *manager* of the branch office.

45. _____

46. Wasn't Eva Hesse's sculpture *stunning?*

46. _____

47. Give *me* the key to your office.

47. _____

48. Most women don't understand *menopause.*

48. _____

49. He tends to be *irresponsible* at times.

49. _____

50. The voters gave their leader a *vote* of confidence in the last election.

50. _____

9. GRAMMAR: COMPLEMENTS

(Study Section 11B, Complement.)

Write the number that tells how the boldface complement is used:

1. **Direct object**
2. **Objective complement (noun)**
3. **Objective complement (adjective)**

4. **subjective complement (noun)**
5. **subjective complement (pronoun)**
6. **subjective complement (adjective)**

Example: Hana is a **nurse.** _____4_____

1. Anne received an anonymous **letter.** 1. _____
2. Jillian was **dejected** after the loss. 2. _____
3. Hiphop lyrics are often real-life **stories.** 3. _____
4. The music sounded **tuneless.** 4. _____
5. Didn't the newspaper provide thorough, accurate **coverage** of that story? 5. _____
6. Prem named Ahmad his **assistant.** 6. _____
7. The judge declared him **insane.** 7. _____
8. Who threw the first **punch?** 8. _____
9. The employment statistics seem **promising.** 9. _____
10. Pat has been a **salesperson.** 10. _____
11. It was **he** who telephoned. 11. _____
12. Close the **door** quietly. 12. _____
13. The news story made us **sad.** 13. _____
14. The experience was **unpleasant.** 14. _____
15. Secondhand smoke is **dangerous.** 15. _____
16. The concert was **lively.** 16. _____
17. She is the construction **manager.** 17. _____
18. I consider her very **rude.** 18. _____
19. He recently bought a **ranch.** 19. _____
20. Canadians are watching less network **television.** 20. _____
21. This had been her **objective.** 21. _____
22. It is **we** who are responsible. 22. _____
23. Consider the **impact** on the campus before voting. 23. _____

24. I denied that it was **I** who called. 24. _____
25. She studies **Japanese** with a tutor. 25. _____
26. We consider her **honest.** 26. _____
27. The haunted house attracted curious **people** from all over. 27. _____
28. He has had great **recognition.** 28. _____
29. The news show commentator finally interviewed the reclusive **pop star.** 29. _____
30. He did not seem particularly **worried.** 30. _____
31. She is **someone** you can trust. 31. _____
32. He enjoys **fishing** in the lake. 32. _____
33. She runs a **marathon** each year. 33. _____
34. This prescription drug is actually a natural **substance.** 34. _____
35. He must have been sound **asleep.** 35. _____
36. Alexandra has no **lack** of intelligence. 36. _____
37. Our interest in his career made him very **happy.** 37. _____
38. Was it **you** who wrote the essay? 38. _____
39. Did you find the **dictionary?** 39. _____
40. Are you the office **manager?** 40. _____
41. Is the victim **anyone** I know? 41. _____
42. The speaker advised **everyone** to use alcohol in moderation. 42. _____
43. The culprit was **neither** of the employees originally suspected. 43. _____
44. His honesty was **impeccable.** 44. _____
45. They made him a good **offer.** 45. _____
46. The voters elected her **judge.** 46. _____

47. The voters elected *her* judge.

47. _____

48. She usually felt *neglected.*

48. _____

49. The chess star considered his opponent *stupid.*

49. _____

50. Elliot convinced *us* completely.

50. _____

10. GRAMMAR: NOUN AND PRONOUN USE

(Study Sections 10–11, Using Nouns, and Section 19, Use the Right Pronoun Case.)

Write the number that tells how each boldface noun or pronoun is used.
Use the first column for the first boldface word, the second column for the second.

1. **subject**	3. **indirect object**	5. **objective complement**	7. **appositive**
2. **direct object**	4. **subjective complement**	6. **object of preposition**	8. **direct address**

Example: The *soldiers* stormed the *beach.*   <u>1</u> <u>2</u>

1. *Debris* from the *wreck* was strewn everywhere.   1. _____ _____

2. Some of his fellow *officers* considered *Benedict* somewhat untrustworthy.   2. _____ _____

3. That must have been the *reason* that she told *us.*   3. _____ _____

4. His unorthodox behavior made *Singer* the *object* of criticism.   4. _____ _____

5. The RCMP appointed *Choi* its chief *agent* for the Western Communities.   5. _____ _____

6. Davita, my *supervisor,* requested a detailed report of the computer labs' *usage* for the fall semester.   6. _____ _____

7. Down the library steps came *Anna,* her arms filled with reference *books.*   7. _____ _____

8. Having completed the test, she put her *paper* on the instructor's *desk* and left.   8. _____ _____

9. There are fourteen *students* whom the dean has named campus *advisors.*   9. _____ _____

10. Because we've made a commitment to improving gender equity on campus, we told the *dean* our *concerns.*   10. _____ _____

11. Brazil's *population* has dramatically shifted from living in the *countryside* to struggling to survive in the urban areas.   11. _____ _____

12. Having bought season *tickets,* I saw *most* of the Senators' games.   12. _____ _____

13. First read the *instructions;* then answer the *questions* carefully.   13. _____ _____

14. Although he knew the *answers* to most of the *questions,* he did not finish the test.   14. _____ _____

15. She gave each *student* an *opportunity* to try out for a part in the play.   15. _____ _____

16. It is, my fellow *students,* time for you to face the *problems* of alcoholism at this college.   16. _____ _____

17. *He* thought about the *day* when he first met her.   17. _____ _____

18. The club *president* invited the members to suggest a *program* for the fall semester.   18. _____ _____

19. My supervisor made *me* head *tutor* for the scholarship program.   19. _____ _____

20. General Wolfe's unorthodox *tactics* bewildered the *enemy.*   20. _____ _____

21. Unless I am misinformed, she considers *herself* a *nonconformist.*   21. _____ _____

22. Dr. Bailey promised *Gary* that the exam would be a fair *challenge.*   22. _____ _____

23. There are, *ladies* and *gentlemen,* many opportunities for safe investments.   23. _____ _____

24. "Wasn't *he* suspended for drinking in the residence *hall?*" asked the Dean of Students.   24. _____ _____

25. We asked the *speaker,* a former Olympic *medalist,* to discuss physical fitness.   25. _____ _____

11. GRAMMAR: NOUN, PRONOUN, AND ADJECTIVE USE

(Study 4–6, The Parts of Speech: A Survey; 10–11, Using Nouns; and 16, Using Adjectives and Adverbs Correctly.)

In the first column, write the number (**1** to **3**) of the **part of speech** of the boldface word. In the second column, write the number (**4** to **9**) that tells how the word is used.

1. noun	4. subject	7. subjective complement
2. pronoun	5. direct object	8. objective complement
3. adjective	6. indirect object	9. object of preposition

Example: Music filled the *air.*   __1__ __5__

1. I lent him some *money.*   1. _____ _____

2. *Mohammed* made the first team.   2. _____ _____

3. I named *her* my successor.   3. _____ _____

4. We elected him *secretary.*   4. _____ _____

5. Duncan has been a commercial *pilot* for ten years.   5. _____ _____

6. The poem was written for *her.*   6. _____ _____

7. The diplomat was *eager* to begin her new position.   7. _____ _____

8. I gave *Elizabeth* a book.   8. _____ _____

9. The report is of interest to *us.*   9. _____ _____

10. Let *us* decide the curriculum.   10. _____ _____

11. Is *he* the star of the show?   11. _____ _____

12. She lives in *Brandon.*   12. _____ _____

13. Willy became *depressed* by all his failures.   13. _____ _____

14. Will *someone* please help me?   14. _____ _____

15. He has many *friends.*   15. _____ _____

16. The Mayor-elect sent *everyone* from his campaign committee an invitation.   16. _____ _____

17. Her story sounds *plausible.*   17. _____ _____

18. Is this *fad* expected to last even six months?   18. _____ _____

19. Keith removed the *books* from his locker.   19. _____ _____

20. The results proved *interesting.*   20. _____ _____

21. *Neither* of the soldiers obeyed the order.   21. _____ _____

22. Give *her* an *A* for effort.   22. _____ _____

23. He became an able *administrator.*   23. _____ _____

24. Can you buy *me* a new car for Valentine's Day?   24. _____ _____

25. The only *way* to survive that course is by reading every day.   25. _____ _____

12. GRAMMAR: VERB TENSE

(Study 14A, Know the Three Principal Parts of the Verb, and 14B, Use the Correct Tense of a Verb.)

Write the number of the **tense** of the boldface verb:

1. present	4. present perfect (*have* or *has*)
2. past	5. past perfect (*had*)
3. future (*shall* or *will*)	6. future perfect (*shall have* or *will have*)

Example: You **spoke** too soon.   2

1. The sun **sets** in the west. 1. ——————

2. He **will** surely **write** us soon. 2. ——————

3. Next summer, we **shall have lived** in this house for ten years. 3. ——————

4. The Wongs **have planted** a vegetable garden. 4. ——————

5. By noon he **will have finished** the whole job. 5. ——————

6. Here **is** the six o'clock news. 6. ——————

7. **Shall** we **reserve** a copy for you? 7. ——————

8. The widow's savings **melted** away. 8. ——————

9. I **had** not **expected** to see her. 9. ——————

10. Carol **sends** her love. 10. ——————

11. The professor **had promised** a delay in the exam. 11. ——————

12. Dylan **will begin** music lessons in the spring. 12. ——————

13. The children **have created** a snow castle in the front yard. 13. ——————

14. **Have** you an extra set of car keys? 14. ——————

15. My eighty-year-old father **loves** to ride his motorcycle on mountain roads. 15. ——————

16. We **painted** the living room a warm shade of yellow. 16. ——————

17. The boys **have saved** their allowances for a special family outing at the circus. 17. ——————

18. The instructor carefully **reviewed** the student's paper before submitting it to the campus magazine. 18. ——————

19. In one week, the flu **hit** five staff members in the office. 19. ——————

20. Michael **has applied** for a fellowship. 20. ——————

In the blank at the right, write the number of the **verb ending,** if any, that should appear at each bracketed space:

0. no ending   1. *s* or *es*   2. *ed* or *d*   3. *ing*

Example: The sun rise[ ] beyond that low hill. 1

The brown cliffs rise[1] directly from the gray sea; no beach come[2] between them. The 1. ——————

waves have pound[3] the granite base of that cliff for ages but have fail[4] to wear[5] it away. 2. ——————

Now, as always, great white gulls circle[6] just above the foam seeking fish that are 3. ——————

destine[7] to become their dinner. Years ago, when I first gather[8] the courage to 4. ——————

approach[9] the cliff's sheer edge and peer[10] over, I imagine[11] what it would be like if I 5. ——————

tumble[12] over and plummet[13] into that seething surf.

I was an imaginative youth, and the thought fascinate[14] me then. At that time I was

try[15] desperately though unsuccessfully to win the heart of a dark-haired local girl, but she

had been continually reject[16] me, and her attitude had turn[17] my thoughts to suicide. I

might, in fact, have hurl[18] myself over the edge, except for one fact. My knees have

always turn[19] to jelly at the mere thought of do[20] it.

Today, as a man of thirty, I can look[21] back on those years and laugh[22]. Yet even

now, whenever I approach[23] that treacherous edge, a chill run[24] through me. It is as if

something inside me is say[25], "Someday you will hurl[26] yourself over. You know[27] it."

I have been haunt[28] by that thought ever since that girl reject[29] me, and I probably will

always be obsess[30] by it—until the end.

6. _____

7. _____

8. _____

9. _____

10. _____

11. _____

12. _____

13. _____

14. _____

15. _____

16. _____

17. _____

18. _____

19. _____

20. _____

21. _____

22. _____

23. _____

24. _____

25. _____

26. _____

27. _____

28. _____

29. _____

30. _____

13. GRAMMAR: VERBS—KIND, VOICE, AND MOOD

(Study Section 13, Know the Kinds of Verbs.)

Write **1** if the boldface verb is **transitive**.
Write **2** if it is **intransitive**.
Write **3** if it is a **linking** verb.

Example: The house *looks* fine. _____3_____

1. Jenny *kissed* me when we met. 1. _____
2. Toby *jogs* for two miles every morning. 2. _____
3. Your laughter *sounds* bitter. 3. _____
4. *Lay* your books on the table. 4. _____
5. The window *opened* onto the bay. 5. _____
6. Dr. Smiley *has* a fine reputation. 6. _____
7. The island *lay* fifty miles off the mainland. 7. _____
8. The last express *has* already *left.* 8. _____
9. The soldier *lay* down between battles. 9. _____
10. The childhood playmates *remained* friends for life. 10. _____
11. The room *smells* smoky. 11. _____
12. The book *seems* too complicated. 12. _____

13. The express *arrived* ten minutes late. 13. _____
14. The mail carrier *left* a package. 14. _____
15. The snow *piled* up into tall, crusty drifts. 15. _____
16. During conversations, speakers often *establish* comfortable social distance through silence. 16. _____
17. The boys *created* valentines for their teachers, friends, and favourite relatives. 17. _____
18. During the first semester, my Asian friend *seemed* nervous because his parents expected good grades. 18. _____
19. The young teacher *was* a former student in my first class. 19. _____
20. Ukrainian women *have been* instrumental in maintaining the social structure of the traditional Ukrainian church. 20. _____

Write **1** if the boldface verb is in the **active** voice.
Write **2** if it is in the **passive** voice.

Example: Lefty *threw* another strike. _____1_____

1. Visitors *are* not *permitted* aboard the aircraft. 1. _____
2. One name *was* inadvertently *omitted* from the list. 2. _____
3. The ambassador *carried* a special agreement to the secret meeting. 3. _____
4. The media *criticized* the Premier's excuse. 4. _____
5. The meeting *was called* to order. 5. _____
6. The ancient city *was* totally *destroyed* by a volcanic eruption. 6. _____
7. An unfortunate error *has been made.* 7. _____

8. Younger voters *have selected* their candidate. 8. _____
9. The witness *faltered* under the vigorous cross-examination. 9. _____
10. The robbery *could have occurred* ab out noon. 10. _____
11. The report *will be submitted* for review next week. 11. _____
12. The left fielder *threw out* the runner. 12. _____
13. Jerry's credit card application *was approved.* 13. _____
14. The star's exercise video *will be sold* through commercials. 14. _____
15. The virus *was* susceptible to heat. 15. _____

Write the number of the *mood* of the boldface verb:

1. indicative   2. imperative   3. subjunctive

Example: If she *were* smart, she'd finish school first.   3

1. The semester **had ended.**   1. _____

2. They **are** colleagues.   2. _____

3. **Kiss** me, you fool!   3. _____

4. The research team **is conducting** another set of experiments.   4. _____

5. Would that I **were** wealthy.   5. _____

6. **Send** my check to the bank.   6. _____

7. If I **were** you, I'd not worry.   7. _____

8. **Drive** carefully without speeding.   8. _____

9. Christina **offered** us some tea.   9. _____

10. Please **read** the directions twice before beginning.   10. _____

11. The students **were** happy about reading break.   11. _____

12. They **were** late as usual.   12. _____

13. **Hurry!**   13. _____

14. The student **hurried** to finish his math test before the end of class.   14. _____

15. If this **be** treason, make the most of it.   15. _____

14. GRAMMAR: VERBALS

(Study Section 14D, Distinguish a Verbal from a Verb.)

Classify **each** boldface verbal:

1. **infinitive**   3. **present participle**
2. **gerund**   4. **past participle**

Example: *To be* or not to be; that is the
    question.   1. __1__

1. Do you like **to watch** football?   1. _____
2. His pastime is **watching** football.   2. _____
3. The Prime Minister's job must be **to restore** the economy for all Canadians.   3. _____
4. Our **talking** distracted him.   4. _____
5. I submitted a **typed** essay.   5. _____
6. **Encouraged** by their initial weight loss, Susan and Roy continued their diets.   6. _____
7. He was eager **to begin.**   7. _____
8. By **hurrying,** he caught the bus.   8. _____

9. **Seeing** us, she smiled.   9. _____
10. She enjoys **driving** sports cars.   10. _____
11. Seismologists continue **to monitor** Vancouver Island for a major earthquake.   11. _____
12. **Examining** the report, the consumer decided not to invest.   12. _____
13. **Frightened,** he became cautious.   13. _____
14. The purpose of the cookbook is **to reduce** the threat of cancer through a healthy diet.   14. _____
15. **Reducing** carbon dioxide emissions was a top priority in the Minister's bill.   15. _____

In the first column, **classify** each boldface verbal:
1. **infinitive**   2. **gerund**

In the second column, write the number that tells how that verbal is used:
1. **subject**   3. **subjective complement**
2. **direct object**   4. **object of preposition**

Example: *Sleeping* until noon is no way to greet the day.   __2__ __1__

1. The professor clearly enjoyed **reading** her favourite passages to the class.   1. _____ _____
2. **To blame** Premier McKenna completely for the weak economy is a rather naive viewpoint.   2. _____ _____
3. Larry likes **working** with young children in summer camp.   3. _____ _____
4. The ambassador's first task was **to arrange** a summit meeting.   4. _____ _____
5. The suspect apparently had no intention of **admitting** the crime.   5. _____ _____
6. Kirsten worried about **borrowing** money.   6. _____ _____
7. We tried **to stop** him from making an unwise decision.   7. _____ _____
8. Her one wish has always been **to travel** throughout Europe.   8. _____ _____
9. **Writing** a letter of application was no problem for her.   9. _____ _____
10. The central characteristic of Inuit discourse is the **monitoring** of the progress of any discussion.   10. _____ _____

15. GRAMMAR: ADJECTIVES AND ADVERBS

(Study Sections 16–17, Using Adjectives and Adverbs.)

Write **1** if the boldface adjective or adverb is used **correctly**.
Write **0** if it is used **incorrectly**.

Example: The Dinosaurs are playing **good** this year. ___0___

1. The sun feels **good.** 1. _____

2. The team shouldn't feel **badly** about losing that game. 2. _____

3. She was the **most** talented member of the pair. 3. _____

4. He keeps in **good** condition always. 4. _____

5. He was very **frank** in his evaluation of her work. 5. _____

6. He spoke very **frankly** with us. 6. _____

7. Of the two students, she is the **smartest.** 7. _____

8. My head aches **bad.** 8. _____

9. The student looked **weary.** 9. _____

10. The student looked **wearily** at the computer monitor. 10. _____

11. I comb my hair **different** now. 11. _____

12. Was Alex hurt **bad?** 12. _____

13. He seemed **real** honest. 13. _____

14. She told **most** everyone the news. 14. _____

15. Reading Alice Munro's work is a **real** pleasure. 15. _____

16. The teaching assistant glanced **nervously** at the class. 16. _____

17. The students seemed **nervous** also. 17. _____

18. The campus will look **differently** when the new buildings are completed. 18. _____

19. Yours is the **clearest** of the two explanations. 19. _____

20. The book is in **good** condition. 20. _____

21. I did **poor** in political science this term. 21. _____

22. Mario looked **great** in his graduation cap and gown. 22. _____

23. Trevor felt **badly** about having to fire the veteran employee. 23. _____

24. Don's excuse was far **more poorer** than Keith's. 24. _____

25. She speaks very **well.** 25. _____

26. It rained **steady** for the whole month of December in Vancouver. 26. _____

27. The roses smell **sweet.** 27. _____

28. He tries **hard** to please everyone. 28. _____

29. John is **near** seven feet tall. 29. _____

30. He talks **considerable** about his future plans. 30. _____

31. She donated a **considerable** sum of money to the project. 31. _____

32. The **smartest** of the twins is spoiled. 32. _____

33. The **smartest** of the triplets is spoiled. 33. _____

34. The coach looked **uneasily** at his players. 34. _____

35. He felt **uneasy** about the score. 35. _____

36. Do try to drive more **careful.** 36. _____

37. It was Bob's **most unique** idea ever. 37. _____

38. The debate was **highly** publicized. 38. _____

39. Judith arrived **considerable** later than the others. 39. _____

40. The street looked **strangely** to us. 40. _____

41. The software has run **good** since the computer viruses were removed from the hard drives. 41. _____

42. He was ill, but he is **well** now. 42. _____

43. That pressure group is the most *influential* in Ottawa.　　43. _____

44. The music sounded *good* throughout the hall.　　44. _____

45. Violence has *really* reached epidemic proportions in this city.　　45. _____

46. He seemed very *serious* about keeping his appointment.　　46. _____

47. The egg rolls smelled *good.*　　47. _____

48. We felt *badly* about missing the farewell party.　　48. _____

49. Rafe looked on *sadly.*　　49. _____

50. Paul was *sad* all morning.　　50. _____

16. GRAMMAR: USING VERBS

(Study Section 15D, Do Not Misuse Irregular Verb Forms.)

Write **1** if the boldface verb is used **correctly.**
Write **0** if it is used **incorrectly;** then write the correct verb form in the second column.

Example: We were *froze* by the time we shoveled the driveway.	0	frozen
1. I *payed* the news carrier.	1. ———	———————
2. We have *flown* home to Newfoundland four times this year.	2. ———	———————
3. In the summer, we *swam* in the creek behind our home.	3. ———	———————
4. The bell in the old Clark Tower has *rang* every evening at 6:00 p.m. for the past fifty years.	4. ———	———————
5. My books *were stolen* when I left them on a table in the library.	5. ———	———————
6. We *have ridden* up that trail many times.	6. ———	———————
7. The little child *tore* open the present wrapped in bright yellow paper.	7. ———	———————
8. The student *sank* into his chair to avoid being called on by the professor.	8. ———	———————
9. We *have gone* to the CNE every year since we moved to Toronto.	9. ———	———————
10. We *should have known* that Robert would not have his portion of the report prepared.	10. ———	———————
11. The little boy standing by the counter *saw* the man shoplift a candy bar.	11. ———	———————
12. Before we realized it, we *had drunk* two pitchers of lemonade.	12. ———	———————
13. My father *rose* at 4:00 a.m. to prepare for his drive to Sarnia.	13. ———	———————
14. The sun *shone* brightly into my bedroom.	14. ———	———————
15. The children *swung* on the swing until their mother called them home for supper.	15. ———	———————
16. When we were small, we *wore* hats and white gloves on special occasions.	16. ———	———————
17. The author *hasn't spoken* to the news media for twenty years.	17. ———	———————
18. Jack *wrote* his essay on the summer spent on his grandfather's farm.	18. ———	———————
19. We *lay* in bed reading the Sunday newspaper and munching donuts.	19. ———	———————
20. Someone *stole* the documentation that accompanied my word processing software.	20. ———	———————

17. GRAMMAR: PRONOUNS—KINDS AND CASE

(Study Section 18, Know the Five Main Kinds of Pronouns, and Section 19, Use the Right Pronoun Case.)

Classify each boldface pronoun:

1. personal pronoun 5. indefinite pronoun
2. interrogative pronoun 6. reflexive pronoun
3. relative pronoun 7. intensive pronoun
4. demonstrative pronoun

Example: *Who* is Sylvia?   2

1. I made him an offer that *he* could not refuse.   1. ____
2. *No one* expected the storm to last so long.   2. ____
3. *This* supports the importance of proper rest when studying for finals.   3. ____
4. He has only *himself* to blame for his predicament.   4. ____
5. *Which* of the political cartoons is the funniest?   5. ____
6. She is the executive *who* makes the key decisions in this company.   6. ____
7. I *myself* have no desire to explore the rough terrain of mountainous regions.   7. ____
8. *Everyone* in the office had access to the safe.   8. ____
9. *Several* of the games went into overtime.   9. ____
10. *Anyone* seeing the documentary must reconsider the issues of residential schools in Canada.   10. ____
11. Dean prepared a speech in case *no one* else was ready to speak.   11. ____
12. These are my biology notes; *those* must be yours.   12. ____
13. *Who* do you think will be the successful candidate in the election?   13. ____
14. *Each* of the victims testified.   14. ____
15. *Neither* of the parties engaged in collective bargaining would budge from its position.   15. ____

Write the number of the **correct** pronoun choice.

Example: Grandpa ordered lunch for Billy and (1) *I* (2) *me.*   2

1. Three of (1) *we* (2) *us* jury members voted for acquittal.   1. ____
2. If you were (1) *I* (2) *me,* would you be willing to increase your holdings in that company?   2. ____
3. May we—John and (1) *I* (2) *me*—join you for the meeting?   3. ____
4. Between you and (1) *I* (2) *me,* I feel quite uneasy about the outcome of the expedition.   4. ____
5. Were you surprised that the trophies were awarded to Julia and (1) *he* (2) *him?*   5. ____
6. It must have been (1) *he* (2) *him* who did the villain's voice for Disney's latest animated feature.   6. ____
7. Why not give (1) *we* (2) *us* students an opportunity to help determine the matter?   7. ____

8. Nobody but (1) *she* (2) *her* can answer that question.   8. _____

9. He is much more talented in dramatics than (1) *she* (2) *her.*   9. _____

10. The Member of Parliament supported (1) *whoever* (2) *whomever* agreed with his ideas for
    reforming Canadian social policy.   10. _____

18. GRAMMAR: PRONOUN CASE

(Study Section 19, Use the Right Pronoun Case.)

In the first column, write the number of the **correct** pronoun choice.
In the second column, write the number of the **reason** for your choice.

Choice	Reasons for Choice
1. subject form (nominative case)	**3. subject of verb**
	4. subjective complement
	5. direct object
2. object form (objective case)	**6. indirect object**
	7. object of preposition
	8. subject of infinitive

	Word Choice	Reason for Choice

Example: Marie studied with Burt and (1) *I* (2) *me*.　　2　　7

1. Do you think it was (1) *she* (2) *her* who poisoned the cocoa?　　1. ___ ___

2. Were you and (1) *he* (2) *him* surprised by the result?　　2. ___ ___

3. Fourteen of (1) *we* (2) *us* students signed a petition to reverse the ruling.　　3. ___ ___

4. The assignment gave (1) *she* (2) *her* no further trouble after it was explained.　　4. ___ ___

5. The author used a chatty, informal style to describe the talk show hosts (1) *who* (2) *whom* she disliked the most.　　5. ___ ___

6. I invited (1) *he* (2) *him* to select topics on which students might speak.　　6. ___ ___

7. Speakers like (1) *she* (2) *her* are both entertaining and informative.　　7. ___ ___

8. I was very much surprised to see (1) *he* (2) *him* at the art exhibit.　　8. ___ ___

9. Are you and (1) *he* (2) *him* both working in the school cafeteria this year?　　9. ___ ___

10. We asked Joan and (1) *he* (2) *him* to supervise the playground activities.　　10. ___ ___

11. The leader of the student group asked, "(1) *Who* (2) *Whom* can afford the 10 percent increase in tuition?"　　11. ___ ___

12. All of (1) *we* (2) *us* newcomers were asked to report for an orientation session.　　12. ___ ___

13. It was (1) *he* (2) *him* who made all the arrangements for the dance.　　13. ___ ___

14. Television network executives seem to think that ratings go to (1) *whoever* (2) *whomever* broadcasts the dumbest shows.　　14. ___ ___

15. My two friends and (1) *I* (2) *me* decided to go on a boat ride around the bay.　　15. ___ ___

16. This argument is just between Dick and (1) *I* (2) *me*.　　16. ___ ___

17. My father always gave (1) *I* (2) *me* money for my tuition.　　17. ___ ___

18. The cowboy movie star from the 1930s offered to do the television special with (1) *whoever* (2) *whomever* promised an accurate portrayal of his life.　　18. ___ ___

19. If you were (1) *I* (2) *me,* would you consider going on a summer cruise?   19. _____ _____

20. Please ask (1) *whoever* (2) *whomever* is at the door to wait.   20. _____ _____

21. Everyone was excused from class except Louise, Mary, and (1) *I* (2) *me.*   21. _____ _____

22. The teaching assistant asked (1) *he* (2) *him* to finish the experiment.   22. _____ _____

23. Nina is as capable as (1) *he* (2) *him* of typing the minutes of the meeting.   23. _____ _____

24. I knew of no one who had encountered more difficulties than (1) *she* (2) *her.*   24. _____ _____

25. Nobody but (1) *he* (2) *him* had been able to qualify for an overseas scholarship.   25. _____ _____

26. The teacher asked (1) *we* (2) *us* to speak extemporaneously on the topic.   26. _____ _____

27. The supervisor is fifteen years younger than (1) *she* (2) *her.*   27. _____ _____

28. Fifty of (1) *we* (2) *us* agreed to raise money for a memorial plaque.   28. _____ _____

29. Are you and (1) *she* (2) *her* planning a joint report?   29. _____ _____

30. Nobody but (1) *he* (2) *him* knows those involved in the scandal.   30. _____ _____

31. I am certain that he is as deserving of praise as (1) *she* (2) *her.*   31. _____ _____

32. If you were (1) *I* (2) *me,* which courses would you select as electives?   32. _____ _____

33. (1) *Who* (2) *Whom* do you think will be the next mayor?   33. _____ _____

34. Assign the task to (1) *whoever* (2) *whomever* is willing to undertake it.   34. _____ _____

35. She is a person (1) *who* (2) *whom* is, without question, destined to achieve success.   35. _____ _____

36. He is the author about (1) *who* (2) *whom* we shall be writing a paper.   36. _____ _____

37. Was it (1) *he* (2) *him* who was questioned about the woman's death?   37. _____ _____

38. The only choice left was between (1) *she* (2) *her* and him.   38. _____ _____

39. No one was critical of the performance but (1) *she* (2) *her.*   39. _____ _____

40. "Were you calling (1) *I* (2) *me?*" Jill asked as she entered the room.   40. _____ _____

41. Both of (1) *we* (2) *us* agreed that the exercise class had been too much for us.   41. _____ _____

42. Imagine finally meeting (1) *he* (2) *him* after so many years of correspondence!   42. _____ _____

43. The sociologist asked the community's matriarch and (1) *she* (2) *her* about the historical significance of quilting in their culture.   43. _____ _____

44. Do you suppose that (1) *he* (2) *him* will ever find time to come?   44. _____ _____

45. Everyone but (1) *she* (2) *her* was there on time.   45. _____ _____

46. It was Gene who hated the movie, not (1) *I* (2) *me.*   46. _____ _____

47. Developing a new school curriculum gave our colleagues and (1) *we* (2) *us* much satisfaction.   47. _____ _____

48. A dispute arose about (1) *who* (2) *whom* would pay the check.   48. _____ _____

49. That executive is the one (1) *who* (2) *whom* initiated the investigation.   49. _____ _____

50. The scholarship will be given to (1) *whoever* (2) *whomever* deserves it most.   50. _____ _____

19. GRAMMAR: PRONOUN REFERENCE

(Study Section 20, Avoid Faulty Reference.)

Write **1** if the boldface word is used **correctly**.
Write **0** if it is used **incorrectly**.

Example: Gulliver agreed with his master that *he* was a Yahoo.   0

1. David won the lottery and quit his job. ***This*** was unexpected   1. _____

2. Betsy told Alison that ***she*** didn't follow through enough.   2. _____

3. Daniel decided to drop out of college. He later regretted ***that*** decision.   3. _____

4. On the white card, list the classes ***that*** you plan to take.   4. _____

5. The billionaire phoned his favourite banker because ***he*** owed him a favour.   5. _____

6. In Quebec, ***they*** eat french fries served with cheese and gravy.   6. _____

7. I was late filing my report, ***which*** greatly embarrassed me.   7. _____

8. On her return from Europe, ***they*** stopped her at Customs.   8. _____

9. She was able to complete college after earning a research assistantship. We greatly admire her
   for ***that.***   9. _____

10. The physician's speech focused on the country's lack of success with the AIDS epidemic; ***it*** was
    not well received.   10. _____

11. The Native Canadian discussed what it means to be a real Indian, ***which*** can be described as
    those who know and respect the ways of their ancestors.   11. _____

12. They planned to climb sheer Mount Maguffey, a feat ***that*** no one had ever accomplished.   12. _____

13. Pat always wanted to be a television newscaster; thus she majored in ***it*** in university.   13. _____

14. Stephenson denounced the use of arbitration in the dispute, ***which*** was not popular with the
    workers.   14. _____

15. ***It*** was well past midnight when the phone rang.   15. _____

16. The speaker kept scratching his head, a mannerism ***that*** proved distracting.   16. _____

17. ***It*** says in the article that the newest artificial sweetener is 10,000 times as sweet as sugar.   17. _____

18. When Lois retires, ***they*** will probably give her a gold watch.   18. _____

19. When Schultz presented his highly negative criticism of the play, the professor said she thought
    it was well written.   19. _____

20. Eric started taking pictures in high school. ***This*** interest led to a brilliant career in photography. 20. _____

21. ***It's*** best that pets be kept outside when family members are allergic to animal dander.   21. _____

22–23. In some vacation spots, ***they*** add the tip to your bill and give poor service. ***This*** isn't the way to   22. _____
       treat a customer.   23. _____

24–25. In some sections of the history text, ***it*** seems as if ***they*** ignored women's contributions to the   24. _____
       development of this country.   25. _____

20. GRAMMAR: PHRASES

(Study 21–22, Recognizing Phrases.)

In the first column, write the number of the **one** set of underlined words that is a **prepositional phrase.**
In the second column, write the number that tells how that phrase is **used** in that sentence:

7. as adjective   **8. as adverb**

Example: <u>The starting pitcher</u> <u>for the Jays</u> is <u>a left-hander.</u>   <u>2</u>   <u>7</u>
              1   2   3

1. <u>When we came downstairs</u>, a cab <u>was awaiting us</u> <u>at the curb.</u>   1. _____ _____
         1   2   3

2. <u>The red-brick building</u> <u>erected in the last century</u> <u>collapsed last week</u> <u>without warning.</u>   2. _____ _____
         1   2   3   4

3. <u>After each session</u>, <u>the noted professor</u> <u>and his assistant</u> answered
         1   2   3

   <u>the audience's questions.</u>   3. _____ _____
         4

4. <u>What they saw</u> <u>before the door closed</u> <u>shocked them</u> <u>beyond belief.</u>   4. _____ _____
         1   2   3   4

5. <u>No one here</u> <u>has ever seen</u> <u>such consummate grace</u> <u>of style</u>.   5. _____ _____
         1   2   3   4

6. <u>The need</u> <u>for adequate child care</u> for dual-income families was not considered
         1   2

   <u>when the Prime Minister addressed the convention.</u>   6. _____ _____
         3

7. <u>The observation</u> <u>that men and women have different courtship rituals</u> seems debatable
         1   2

   <u>in a modern postindustrial society.</u>   7. _____ _____
         3

8. <u>An issue</u> <u>like pornography</u> <u>can really upset</u> even the most liberal community.   8. _____ _____
         1   2   3

9. <u>Until 10,000 years ago</u>, <u>all humans</u> relied on food gathering and hunting
         1   2

   <u>to maintain their existence.</u>   9. _____ _____
         3

10. <u>Through extended negotiations</u> <u>the disputing parties</u> <u>reached an agreement</u>
          1   2

    <u>that had long seemed impossible.</u>   10. _____ _____
          3

If the words in boldface are **a verbal phrase** (infinitive, gerund, or participial), write **1** in the first column and one of the following numbers in the second column:

2. verbal phrase used as **adjective**
3. verbal phrase used as **adverb**
4. verbal phrase used as **noun**

If the boldface words **are not a verbal phrase,** write **0** in the first column and nothing in the second column.

Example: *Singing in the rain* is a sure way to get wet. <u>1</u> <u>4</u>

Example: Gene is *singing in the rain* despite his cold. <u>0</u> <u>   </u>

1. *Taking portrait photographs of pets* is her means of earning a living. 1. _____ _____

2. These days she is *taking portrait photographs of pets* as her means of earning a living. 2. _____ _____

3. *To analyze the problem,* Susan created a list of both the advantages and disadvantages. 3. _____ _____

4. By age thirty, many women begin *sensing a natural maternal need.* 4. _____ _____

5. A successful high school athlete, *courted by major universities,* sometimes receives substantial cash gifts from athletic booster clubs. 5. _____ _____

6. English departments have debated the issue of *forsaking a Eurocentric curriculum* for a more multicultural approach. 6. _____ _____

7. His idea of a thrill is *driving in stock-car races.* 7. _____ _____

8. *Driving in stock-car races,* he not only gets his thrills but also earns prize money. 8. _____ _____

9. Nowadays he is *driving in stock-car races* for thrills and money. 9. _____ _____

10. He would like *to spend his life* as a race driver. 10. _____ _____

37

21. GRAMMAR: VERBAL PHRASES

(Study Section 22, The Verbal Phrase.)

Classify each boldface verbal phrase:

1. **infinitive phrase** used as noun
2. **infinitive phrase** used as adjective
3. **infinitive phrase** used as adverb
4. **present participle phrase**
5. **past participle phrase**
6. **gerund phrase**

(Use the first column for the first phrase, the second column for the second.)

Example: ***Thrilled by her results,*** Elaine began ***applying to several colleges.***   5 ___ 6 ___

1. ***Seeing the traffic worsen,*** Adam chose ***to wait until after rush hour.***   1. ___ ___

2. ***Obtaining a ticket at that late hour*** was not easy ***to do.***   2. ___ ___

3. ***Controlling acid rain*** is a crucial step in ***protecting our lakes and rivers.***   3. ___ ___

4. ***Intrigued by what he was saying,*** she forgot ***to go to her science class.***   4. ___ ___

5. ***Knowing his potential,*** I agreed that John was the man ***to select for the position.***   5. ___ ___

6. ***To provide economic growth*** is the mayor's first task ***facing her after inauguration.***   6. ___ ___

7. I can't help ***admiring her;*** did you object to ***my praising her work?***   7. ___ ___

8. I appreciate ***your helping us;*** will you be able ***to help us again?***   8. ___ ___

9. ***Loaded down with library books,*** she tried ***to open the front door.***   9. ___ ___

10. ***Preparing his history assignment*** was not as hard ***to do*** as he had anticipated.   10. ___ ___

11. ***Considering the link between non-Hodgkins lymphoma and hair dyeing products,*** many women may decide ***to keep their natural hair colour.***   11. ___ ___

12. Luc tried ***to run the whole mile,*** but he was too tired ***to do more than a single lap.***   12. ___ ___

13. The speaker, ***obviously resenting our interruptions,*** frowned at us as we tried ***to ask other questions.***   13. ___ ___

14. ***Hiking over mountain trails*** is a sport ***demanding endurance.***   14. ___ ___

15. The hunter put down his gun, realizing ***that the ducks had flown out of range*** and ***wishing to save ammunition.***   15. ___ ___

16. To try to pass the test without ***studying for it*** was not a wise thing ***to do.***   16. ___ ___

17. ***Alarmed by the rapid spread of the measles epidemic,*** the health authorities had no alternative but ***to vaccinate as many children as possible.***   17. ___ ___

18. ***Feeling guilty about working outside of the home,*** the young mother planned ***to spend time with her children every Saturday.***   18. ___ ___

19. ***Drinking chlorinated water*** may be linked to ***increasing the risk of bladder cancer.***   19. ___ ___

20. She tried t***o obtain the information*** without ***asking any direct questions.***   20. ___ ___

21. The student **waiting in your office** has **to select a major this semester.**   21. _____ _____

22. **Careless campers** have been the cause of too many forests **being reduced to ashes.**   22. _____ _____

23. By **looking carefully**, he found an article that was easy **to understand**.   23. _____ _____

24. **Obviously surprised by the sacrifices required**, Kelly reconsidered whether she wanted **to begin gymnastic training for the next Olympics.**   24. _____ _____

25. **To be extremely safe,** physicians are recommending that patients **preparing for any surgery donate blood**.   25. _____ _____

22. GRAMMAR: PHRASES—REVIEW

(Study Sections 21–22, Recognizing Phrases.)
In the first column, **classify** each boldface phrase:

1. **prepositional phrase**   4. **gerund phrase**
2. **infinitive phrase**   5. **absolute phrase**
3. **participle phrase**

In the second column, tell how that phrase is used:

6. **as adjective**   7. **as adverb**   8. **as noun**

(For an absolute phrase, write nothing in the second column.)

Example: The orders came *from on high.*   <u>1</u>   <u>7</u>

1. The woman standing *between the delegates* is an interpreter.   1. ____ ____

2. The woman *standing between the delegates* is an interpreter.   2. ____ ____

3. Emily looked for her zither everywhere *around the house.*   3. ____ ____

4. *His insisting that he was right* made him unpopular with his associates.   4. ____ ____

5. The committee voted *to adjourn immediately.*   5. ____ ____

6. *Because of the storm,* the excursion around the lake had to be postponed. 6. ____ ____

7. *To be the president of the club* pleased him very much.   7. ____ ____

8. *During July and August,* many people go on vacation trips.   8. ____ ____

9. *Flying a jet at supersonic speeds* has been Sally's dream since childhood. 9. ____ ____

10. The agent *wearing an official badge* is the one to see about tickets.   10. ____ ____

11. *Realizing that his back injury would get worse,* the star player retired from
    professional basketball.   11. ____ ____

12. *To help reduce public dissatisfaction with the monarchy,* Queen Elizabeth has
    pledged to pay her share of taxes.   12. ____ ____

13. *To assist students with their course schedules,* counselors will be on duty all day. 13. ____ ____

14. Garth was successful in *producing a long succession of hit shows.*   14. ____ ____

15. *The semester almost over,* students were packing up to go home.   15. ____ ____

16. The distinguished-looking man *in the blue suit* is the head of the company. 16. ____ ____

17. *Earning a college degree* used to guarantee a good-paying job.   17. ____ ____

18. Approximately one-third *of the Canadian work force* has had some post–secondary
    education.   18. ____ ____

19. Their ears were attuned *to any unusual sound.*   19. ____ ____

20. I would appreciate *your letting us know your time of arrival.*   20. ____ ____

21. Two crates *of oranges* were delivered to the residence.   21. ____ ____

22. *Anticipating an overflow audience,* the janitor put extra chairs in the auditorium.   22. _____ _____

23. A car *filled with students* left early this morning to arrange for the class picnic.   23. _____ _____

24. I cannot help *thinking that he might have done better in the test.*   24. _____ _____

25. We were obliged to abandon our plans, *the boat having been damaged in a recent storm.*   25. _____ _____

26. We knew, *conditions being what they were,* that further progress was impossible.   26. _____ _____

27. *Doing my homework* interfered with my watching television.   27. _____ _____

28. *Waving his arms and shouting,* John threatened everyone in the courtroom.   28. _____ _____

29. *Flipping through the channels,* Fred decided that reading the phone book would be more interesting then watching television.   29. _____ _____

30. *Her experiment having been completed,* she left the science building and went home.   30. _____ _____

31. Scientists are using artificial life simulation programs *for futuristic experimentation.*   31. _____ _____

32. *Scandalized by certain television commercials that seem to promote sex and little else,* Jane decided to write letters to the companies with the most offensive ads.   32. _____ _____

33. *Realizing that the Broadway tickets would be over $100,* John and Tina decided to see a movie instead.   33. _____ _____

34. *Backing up all files* was something she seldom did.   34. _____ _____

35. *Resisting the latest military coup attempt,* the small South American country may have proven that civilian leaders will have a chance to govern.   35. _____ _____

36. Canada, the US, Asia, and Europe now appear *to be threatened by ozone holes in the atmosphere.*   36. _____ _____

37. The international community, *changing with the fall of the Soviet Union,* has revamped its undercover operations.   37. _____ _____

38. More Canadian military bases will be closed because of cuts *in the defense budget.*   38. _____ _____

39. *Growing tired of the violence and sex in most movies,* many parents' groups are protesting at local theatres.   39. _____ _____

40. Almost eighty percent of those Canadians *polled recently* believed that with enough determination and talent, anyone can be successful in this country.   40. _____ _____

41. *Being part of an extended family* is important to many Inuit societies.   41. _____ _____

42. As societies become more industrialized, the benefits *of raising small families* outweigh having large families.   42. _____ _____

43. *In 1956,* sex education became compulsory in Swedish public schools.   43. _____ _____

44. *To understand Japanese productivity,* observers must appreciate the importance of group achievement to Japanese culture.   44. _____ _____

45. *Consuming more than 50 pounds of ground beef each year,* Americans annually buy 6.7 billion hamburger patties at fast-food restaurants.   45. _____ _____

46. *The weekend ruined,* Lawrence decided to go to bed early even though he had more schoolwork to complete.   46. _____ _____

47. Canadian widows, *reporting that friends and relatives interfere too much,* frequently prefer to spend time alone.   47. _____ _____

48. Anthropologists explain cultural variations *by discussing the impact that ecological and societal functions have on people.*   48. _____ _____

49. **To demonstrate a sense of humility** is important in verbal communication among Chinese speakers.

49. _____ _____

50. **Shouting at his roommate,** James stalked off to sleep at a friend's house.

50. _____ _____

23. GRAMMAR: CLAUSES

(Study Sections 23–25, Recognizing Clauses.)
Classify each boldface clause:

1. independent (main) clause   2. adjective clause
                                              3. adverb clause   } dependent (subordinate) clauses
                                               4. noun clause

Example: Do the dishes *when you're finished eating.*   3

1. Day-care employees complain *because there's no economic incentive to stay in the field.*   1. _____

2. The Premier considered the latest proposal, *which called for local politicians to suggest ways of cutting the deficit.*   2. _____

3. Late-night viewers know *how the talk–show host always begins his monologue.*   3. _____

4. The student *who made the top grade in the history quiz* is my roommate.   4. _____

5. *Whether I am able to go to university* depends on whether I can find a job.   5. _____

6. *After Joe had written a paper for his English class,* he watched television.   6. _____

7. *While I waited for a bus,* I chatted with friends.   7. _____

8. The college counseling centre offers help to anyone *who needs it.*   8. _____

9. There is much excitement *whenever election results are announced.*   9. _____

10. Medical research has made incredible progress with the problems of infertility, *but little is actually known about menopause.*   10. _____

11. Few Canadians realize *that seven percent of psychiatrists admit to unethical behaviour with their clients.*   11. _____

12. My first impression was *that someone had been in my room quite recently.*   12. _____

13. The actress *who had lost the Oscar* declared through clenched teeth that she was delighted just to have been nominated.   13. _____

14. He dropped a letter in the mailbox; *then he went to the library.*   14. _____

15. The candidate's decision to withdraw from the city council race occurred *because she didn't approve of the media's treatment of her mental illness.*   15. _____

16. Why don't you sit here *until the rest of the class arrives?*   16. _____

17. The real estate mogul, *who is not known for his modesty,* has named yet another parking lot after himself.   17. _____

18. *Although he is fifty-two years old,* he is very youthful in appearance.   18. _____

19. Employees of Euro Disney in central France complained bitterly *when they were confronted with Disney's strict employment manual.*   19. _____

20. She lived on a ranch *when she was in Alberta.*   20. _____

21. *Why don't you wait* until you have all the facts?   21. _____

22. She is a person *whom everyone respects and admires.*   22. _____

23. The weather is surprisingly warm *even though it is December.*   23. _____

24. I said nothing except *that I had been unavoidably detained.*   24. _____

25. Voters were disgusted with the House of Commons *because its members had excessive pensions.*   25. _____

26. The trophy will be awarded to *whoever wins the contest.*   26. _____

27. The detective walked up the stairs; *he opened the door of the guest room.*   27. _____

28. Is this the book *that you asked us to order for you?*   28. _____

29. Most voters found it hard to believe *that the public has paid over $80,000 for the moving expenses of the new Chair.*   29. _____

30. The "wanna-be" millionaires had no idea *what the investment seminar would cover during the three-day program.*   30. _____

31. *Because researchers discovered that elementary teachers do not always pay sufficient attention to individual students during reading lessons,* many principals are encouraging innovative language arts programs.   31. _____

32. Societies *which exist in severe surroundings* often enjoy games of chance such as cockfighting.   32. _____

33. Most Canadians realize *that dual-income families are a result of a declining economy rather than gender equality.*   33. _____

24. GRAMMAR: CLAUSES

(Study Section 24, Kinds of Dependent Clauses.)

Identify the **dependent** clause in each sentence by writing its first and last words in the first two columns; in the third column, classify it as:

1. **noun**
2. **adjective**
3. **adverb**

Example: The band was dividing the money when the police arrived. | when | arrived | 3

1. Although most Canadians want better medical services, over fifty percent complain about high taxes.
   1. _____ _____ __

2. The citizens of the war-torn city search each day for a place where the gunfire won't reach them.
   2. _____ _____ __

3. Children caught in an angry divorce case are bound to suffer some anxiety because their parents have a tense relationship with each other.
   3. _____ _____ __

4. The student who complained about the food was given another dessert.
   4. _____ _____ __

5. Whether Camille dyes her hair remains a mystery.
   5. _____ _____ __

6. After Jonathan had read the morning paper, he threw up his hands in despair.
   6. _____ _____ __

7. While I waited for Jesse, I was able to finish my crossword puzzle.
   7. _____ _____ __

8. Professor George gave extra help to anyone who asked for it.
   8. _____ _____ __

9. There is always a lot of anxiety whenever exams are held.
   9. _____ _____ __

10. The coach decided that I was not going to play that year.
    10. _____ _____ __

11. Once more, I waited until I had only one night to write my essay.
    11. _____ _____ __

12. Dr. Jackson, who prided himself on his fairness, declared Burton the winner.
    12. _____ _____ __

13. Because the snow continued to fall quite steadily, the party was postponed.
    13. _____ _____ __

14. I'll never forget Legree's face when I told him to leave.
    14. _____ _____ __

15. Allen remarked that he too had trouble with calculus.
    15. _____ _____ __

16. It was the only mistake that I had ever seen Henning make.
    16. _____ _____ __

17. Nathan explained how his concern about its electrical system kept him from buying the car.
    17. _____ _____ __

18. Most of the audience had tears in their eyes when Juliet died.
    18. _____ _____ __

19. British Columbia, which permits clear–cutting, also charges relatively low stumpage fees.
    19. _____ _____ __

20. The candidate told his followers that he could spend one million dollars a week on the campaign.
    20. _____ _____ __

25. GRAMMAR: NOUN AND ADJECTIVE CLAUSES

(Study Section 24A, An Adjective Clause, and Section 24C, A Noun Clause.)
Classify each boldface dependent clause:

Noun Clause		Adjective Clause
1. used as subject	3. used as subjective complement	5. nonrestrictive (nonessential)
2. used as direct object	4. used as object of preposition	6. restrictive (essential)

Example: *That she was incompetent* was clear.   1

1. *Who was the better skier* remained unresolved.   1. _____

2. The programmer *who wrote the new computer game* retired at twenty.   2. _____

3. I don't see how anyone could object to *what the speaker said.*   3. _____

4. The lab assistant gave the disk to Joan, *whom he had helped to learn the word processing software.*   4. _____

5. *What he wanted us to do for him* seemed utterly impossible.   5. _____

6. Give the four books to *whoever is going to the library.*   6. _____

7. Large classes and teacher apathy are problems *that most schools tend to ignore.*   7. _____

8. A teacher's worst fear is *that her students will hate to read.*   8. _____

9. Laura is a person *who seems to thrive on hard work.*   9. _____

10. Animal rights activists demonstrated in provinces *where grizzly bear hunting is still allowed.*   10. _____

11. Samuel F. B. Morse, *who is famous for his promotion of the telegraph,* was also a successful portrait painter.   11. _____

12. Children learn sexual identity by *how their parents introduce gender roles.*   12. _____

13. The long, black limousine, *which had been waiting in front of the building,* sped away suddenly.   13. _____

14. At the time of Columbus's voyage to America, there were over three hundred Native American tribes, *which accounted for over a million people.*   14. _____

15. *What you decide to do now* is critically important.   15. _____

16. The woman *who wrote this letter* shows remarkable perspicacity.   16. _____

17. The lotto will be won by *whoever holds the lucky numbers.*   17. _____

18. Naphtha, *which is highly flammable,* is no longer much used for dry cleaning.   18. _____

19. Corporate spies claim *that bribing employees is the easiest way to acquire information.*   19. _____

20. The alarm sounded at a moment *when the students were seated in the gymnasium.*   20. _____

21. We were appalled by *what he had to tell us regarding the episode.*   21. _____

22. *That the war was already lost* could no longer be denied.   22. _____

23. The Black Hills is the site *where paleontologists unearthed the most complete Tyrannosaurus rex ever found.*   23. _____

24. Len enrolled in astronomy, a subject ***that had always appealed to him.*** 24. _____

25. The truth is ***that she had studied the wrong chapter.*** 25. _____

26. GRAMMAR: ADVERB CLAUSES

(Study Section 24B, An Adverb Clause.)
Classify each boldface adverb clause:

1. time (*when, after, until,* etc.)   6. condition (*if, unless,* etc.)
2. place (*where, wherever*)   7. concession (*although, though*)
3. manner (*as, as if, as though*)   8. result (*that*)
4. cause (*because, since*)   9. degree or comparison (*as, than*)
5. purpose (*that, so that,* etc.)

Example: There would be a recount *if I had my way.*   <u> 6 </u>

1. *Because pigs are used in Europe to sniff for truffles,* pot-bellied Vietnamese pigs are now being trained to detect illegal drugs in many countries.   1. _____

2. The candidate was willing to speak *wherever she could find an audience.*   2. _____

3. Bruni ran *as if his life depended on it.*   3. _____

4. She has always been able to read much faster *than her brother has.*   4. _____

5. *If I were you,* I would not ask for special consideration at this time.   5. _____

6. Multinational cigarette companies plan to develop markets in Japan *so that they can take advantage of the increase in Japanese smokers.*   6. _____

7. Most of the audience left *before the concert was half over.*   7. _____

8. People are said to be only as old *as they think they are.*   8. _____

9. He read extensively *in order that he might be well prepared for the test.*   9. _____

10. *Unless the Canadian economy changes,* small family farms will soon disappear.   10. _____

11. *Although his grades were satisfactory,* he did not qualify for the scholarship.   11. _____

12. She had worried so much *that she could no longer function effectively.*   12. _____

13. *Whether you are selected,* you will be notified.   13. _____

14. *Because farmers were given more money for their crops,* food prices will increase significantly for consumers.   14. _____

15. She was so excited *that she had trouble going to sleep that night.*   15. _____

16. Do not complete the rest of the form *until you have seen your adviser.*   16. _____

17. *Although Mugsy was only 5 feet 5 inches tall,* he was determined to be a basketball star.   17. _____

18. *Even though fax machines are convenient,* their technology increases the chance that a company will be victimized by corporate spies.   18. _____

19. Robert preferred to go *where no one would recognize him.*   19. _____

20. *When the litmus paper turns red,* the substance is an acid.   20. _____

21. Andre hit the ball so far *that it landed on Waveland Avenue.*   21. _____

22. She usually received better grades *than her brother did.*   22. _____

23. Ethnic jokes can be particularly harmful *since such humour subtly reinforces stereotypes.*   23. _____

24. The actor would not believe the positive reviews of his movies **unless his own mother agreed with the reviewers.**   24. _____

25. She smiled **as if she knew something not known to the rest of us.**   25. _____

27 GRAMMAR: KINDS OF SENTENCES

(Study Section 25, Clauses in Sentences.)

Classify each sentence:

1. simple   2. compound   3. complex   4. compound-complex

(Subordinate clauses in the first ten sentences are in boldface.)

Example: He opened the throttle, and the boat sped off. _2_

1. Mr. Taylor still insisted *that he was an excellent driver.* 1. _____

2. The king, *who was scornful of his advisers,* declared war; he soon regretted his rashness. 2. _____

3. Completion of campus buildings will be delayed *unless funds become available.* 3. _____

4. Consider the matter carefully *before you decide;* your decision will be final. 4. _____

5. This year, either medical companies or discount store chains will be a good investment for the average small investor. 5. _____

6. *The Adventures of Huckleberry Finn,* written by Mark Twain, has been wrongly criticized by some for racist attitudes. 6. _____

7. The storm, *which had caused much damage,* subsided; we then continued on our hike. 7. _____

8. We waited *until all the spectators had left the gymnasium.* 8. _____

9. The site for the theatre having been selected, construction was begun. 9. _____

10. Ontario public schools face an enormous task educating their children; almost 100 languages are spoken by students in these schools. 10. _____

11. His career as a spy being ended, he settled in Manitoba and began writing his memoirs. 11. _____

12. The populations of industrialized nations are growing slowly, and, therefore, the economies of these countries are on the decline. 12. _____

13. His chief worry was that he might reveal the secret by talking in his sleep. 13. _____

14. Many immigrant children speak neither English nor French when they enter school; kindergarten teachers, therefore, must have special training to succeed. 14. _____

15. The story that appeared in the school paper contained several inaccuracies. 15. _____

16. The police officer picked up the package and inspected it carefully. 16. _____

17. Because she was eager to get an early start, Sue packed the night before. 17. _____

18. Experts estimate that there will be 100,000 Canadians 100 years or older by 2080; this significant increase of centenarians will certainly have an impact on healthcare policy. 18. _____

19. Noticing the late arrivals, the speaker motioned for them to be seated. 19. _____

20. A study of over 50 centenarians revealed that most of the subjects had a satisfying relationship with a family member or care provider; in other words, these older Canadians were not lonely in their old age. 20. _____

21. The suspect went to the police station and turned himself in. 21. _____

22. The Sierra Club will fight against any agreement that allows forest companies to cut down ancient British Columbian forests. 22. _____

23. Her father, who is an amateur photographer, won a prize in a recent contest. 23. _____

24. Members of Parliament have had many perks reduced, including subsidized hair cuts and meals. 24. _____

25. The house that we wanted was sold; consequently, we had to look for another one. 25. _____

26. Scientists from all over the world convened to discuss the increasingly serious problem of the greenhouse effect. 26. _____

27. In the 1990s, Canadian are stressing their diverse cultural and ethnic heritage; not everyone agrees this is good for the country. 27. _____

28. Many Japanese women with professional careers are declining to marry Japanese men, whom they find boring, old-fashioned, and too demanding. 28. _____

29. Incredibly, we are paying high prices to buy software that performs simple tasks, such as balancing checkbooks. 29. _____

30. Although Amy's choreography won praise from the critics, she wasn't satisfied, so she spent the next morning reworking it, 30. _____

31. Did she appear tired? 31. _____

32. A computer company recently announced a personal digital assistant, which is essentially a computerized notepad. 32. _____

33. Robert Scully hosts both an English language TV show, "Venture," and a French language one, *"Scully Recontre."* 33. _____

34. Among wealthy nations, Japan is the only country that has a lower personal income tax than the United States. 34. _____

35. The hope of Canadian unity seems distant to many Canadians having difficulty satisfying the demands of Quebec nationalists. 35. _____

36. Most artwork represents forms found in real life; in other words, it is the artist's job to represent familiar shapes through elements pleasing to a particular culture. 36. _____

37. Couples marrying before the age of thirty experience a high divorce rate. 37. _____

38. Banks promise their customers that banking will become increasingly more convenient through computer technology. 38. _____

39. In our community, a vocational centre has established a resettlement for refugees. 39. _____

40. Ethnographers describe the public communications styles of English–speaking Canadians as more subdued than those of French–speaking Canadians. 40. _____

41. All the student organizations pledged to help fund a multicultural centre, for everyone recognized the importance of developing more effective communication among the various cultural groups on campus. 41. _____

42. Evan smacked his lips and plowed through another stack of buttermilk pancakes smothered in blueberry syrup. 42. _____

43. In Alberta, we love our steaks thick and rare. 43. _____

44. Because of his high spirits, David had to endure the nickname of Crash when he was a little boy. 44. _____

45. Maria's parents forbade her from dating without an appropriate chaperon; however, she managed to steal a few moments alone with her boyfriend Saturday morning. 45. _____

46. The women sat up late one night talking about their first dates; most laughed about their awkward teenage years. 46. _____

47. Most reading theorists describe reading as an interactive process between the reader and the text. 47. _____

48. When Holly stepped into my office and whispered a conspiratorial "Guess what," I knew that I was about to be treated to a juicy bit of gossip.

48. _____

49. In recent years, a great number of inquiries have helped Canadians learn about the shocking conditions at residential schools.

49. _____

50. The English Department's faculty and graduate students have proposed guidelines for nonsexist language.

50. _____

28. GRAMMAR: AGREEMENT—SUBJECT AND VERB

(Study Section 26, Make Every Verb Agree with Its Subject in Person and Number.)

Write the number of the correct choice.

Example: One of my favourite programs (1) *was* (2) *were* canceled.   1 ____

1. Neither the researcher nor the subject (1) *has* (2) *have* any idea which is the placebo.   1. _____

2. Economics (1) *is* (2) *are* what the students are most interested in.   2. _____

3. Dialing a 900 number to seek medical emergency information and recommendations (1) *has* (2) *have* been a recent technological advancement.   3. _____

4. Not one of the nominees (1) *has* (2) *have* impressed me.   4. _____

5. (1) *Does* (2) *Do* each of the questions count the same number of points?   5. _____

6. The number of jobs lost in Atlantic Canada's fisheries (1) *has* (2) *have* increased significantly in the past two years.   6. _____

7. Ninety-nine (1) *is* (2) *are* hyphenated because it is a compound number.   7. _____

8. The Prime Minister, along with a dozen RCMP bodyguards, (1) *was* (2) *were* to arrive by noon.   8. _____

9. Both the secretary and the treasurer (1) *was* (2) *were* asked to submit reports.   9. _____

10. Everyone in the auditorium (1) *was* (2) *were* startled by the announcement.   10. _____

11. *Women* (1) *is* (2) *are* a common noun, plural in number.   11. _____

12. Every kindergarten student and first-grader (1) *was* (2) *were* expected to report to the gymnasium.   12. _____

13. There (1) *is* (2) *are* a professor, several students, and a teaching assistant meeting to discuss the course reading list.   13. _____

14. Ten dollars (1) *is* (2) *are* too much to pay for that book.   14. _____

15. (1) *Is* (2) *Are* there any computers available in the lab this morning?   15. _____

16. Neither the professor nor his teacher assistant (1) *has* (2) *have* my missing essay.   16. _____

17. Each of the problems now (1) *needs* (2) *need* the Chair's immediate attention.   17. _____

18. (1) *Is* (2) *Are* your father and brother coming to see you graduate tomorrow?   18. _____

19. A typewriter and a sheet of paper (1) *was* (2) *were* all that he needed at the moment.   19. _____

20. There (1) *is* (2) *are* just one chocolate and two vanilla cookies left in my lunch box.   20. _____

21. (1) *Does* (2) *Do* Coach Jasek and the players know about the special award?   21. _____

22. My two weeks' vacation (1) *was* (2) *were* filled with many projects around the house.   22. _____

23. The only thing that annoyed the speaker (1) *was* (2) *were* the frequent interruptions.   23. _____

24. (1) *Hasn't* (2) *Haven't* either of the officers submitted a written statement?   24. _____

25. The news of his spectacular achievements (1) *comes* (2) *come* as a surprise to all of us.   25. _____

26. On the table (1) *was* (2) *were* a pen, a pad of paper, and two rulers.   26. _____

27. It's remarkable that the entire class (1) *is* (2) *are* passing this summer.   27. _____

28. It (1) *was* (2) *were* a book and a disk that disappeared from the desk.   28. _____

29. There (1) *is* (2) *are* many opportunities for part-time employment on campus.   29. _____

30. (1) *Is* (2) *Are* algebra and chemistry required courses?   30. _____

31. One of his three instructors (1) *has* (2) *have* offered to write a letter of recommendation.   31. _____

32. (1) *Does* (2) *Do* either of the books have a section on usage rules?   32. _____

33. Neither the leading gymnast from Canada nor the star gymnast from the Unified Team (1) *was* (2) *were* able to fulfill her dream of winning an Olympic gold medal.   33. _____

34. Parades, costumes, and music (1) *is* (2) *are* all part of the pre-Lenten carnival celebrated in Trinidad and Tobago.   34. _____

35. Each of the books (1) *has* (2) *have* an introduction written by the author's mentor.   35. _____

36. A special family dinner New Year's Eve and exchange of gifts and parades (1) *describes* (2) *describe* how many Chinese-Canadians celebrate their Lunar New Year.   36. _____

37. Neither the teacher nor the parents (1) *understands* (2) *understand* why Nathan does so well in math but can barely read first-grade books.   37. _____

38. The old woman who walks the twin Scottish terriers (1) *detests* (2) *detest* small children running on the sidewalk in front of her house.   38. _____

39. At the Boy Scout camp out, eggs and bacon (1) *was* (2) *were* the first meal the troop attempted to prepare on an open fire.   39. _____

40. There (1) *is* (2) *are* language, social relations, interests, and geographical origins to help define cultural groups.   40. _____

41. Everyone (1) *was* (2) *were* planning a spring break escape because of the dreary, wet, cold February weather.   41. _____

42. The children, along with their teacher, (1) *is* (2) *are* preparing a one-act play for the spring open house.   42. _____

43. Hartley Olson is one of those people who (1) *complains* (2) *complain* about public school education without volunteering to help make it better.   43. _____

44. Lucy announced that *The Holy Terrors* (1) *is* (2) *are* the title of her next book, which is about raising her three sons.   44. _____

45. The Mohawk tribes of Ontario along with many others (1) *honours* (2) *honour* each season of the year with a special celebration.   45. _____

46. Five dollars (1) *do* (2) *does* not seem like much to my eight-year-old son.   46. _____

47. Either the choir members or the organist (1) *was* (2) *were* constantly battling with the minister about purchasing fancy new choir robes.   47. _____

48. In the last one hundred years, millions of people from all over the world (1) *has* (2) *have* left their homelands to immigrate to the Canada.   48. _____

49. Food from different geographic locations and ethnic groups often (1) *helps* (2) *help* distinguish specific cultural events.   49. _____

50. Even if Canadians' ancestors came here many decades ago, everyone living in this country (1) *has* (2) *have* a specific cultural background.   50. _____

29. GRAMMAR: AGREEMENT—SUBJECT AND VERB

(Study Section 26, Make Every Verb Agree with Its Subject in Person and Number.)

Write the number of the correct choice.

Example: Neither Sarah nor her parents (1) *was* (2) *were* ready to leave the fairgrounds.　　2

1. Virtually every painting and every sculpture Picasso did (1) *is* (2) *are* worth over a million dollars.　1. _____

2. There on the table (1) *was* (2) *were* my wallet and my key chain.　2. _____

3. Neither the documentary about beekeeping nor the two shows about Iceland (1) *was* (2) *were* successful in the ratings.　3. _____

4. Each of the young authors (1) *hopes* (2) *hope* to publish within the next five years.　4. _____

5. Sitting on the stairway (1) *was* (2) *were* the instructor and four of her students.　5. _____

6. *Les Atrides* (1) *is* (2) *are* a ten-hour, four-play production of ancient Greek theatre.　6. _____

7. A political convention, with its candidates, delegates, and reporters, (1) *seems* (2) *seem* like bedlam.　7. _____

8. In the auditorium (1) *was* (2) *were* gathered many students to honour the new officers.　8. _____

9. Each of the art historians (1) *has* (2) *have* offered a theory for why the Leonardo painting has such a stark background.　9. _____

10. (1) *Was* (2) *Were* either President Smith or Dean Nicholson asked to speak at the awards ceremony?　10. _____

11. High-powered cars (1) *has* (2) *have* become his main interest in life.　11. _____

12. His baseball and his glove (1) *was* (2) *were* all Roberto was permitted to take to the game.　12. _____

13. Neither my friends nor I (1) *expects* (2) *expect* to go on the overnight trip.　13. _____

14. My coach and mentor (1) *is* (2) *are* Mr. Graham.　14. _____

15. *Chatelaine*, along with *Toronto Life*, (1) *has* (2) *have* had a woman editor.　15. _____

16. The researcher, as well as her assistants, (1) *is* (2) *are* developing a study to compare the brain tissue of Alzheimer sufferers and healthy subjects.　16. _____

17. Neither criticism nor frequent failures (1) *was* (2) *were* enough to retard his progress.　17. _____

18. Where (1) *is* (2) *are* the end of the recession and the beginning of economic recovery?　18. _____

19. She is the only one of six candidates who (1) *refuses* (2) *refuse* to speak at the ceremony.　19. _____

20. Neither the officer nor the spectators (1) *was* (2) *were* certain of the robber's identity.　20. _____

21. Economics (1) *has* (2) *have* been the most dismal science I've ever studied.　21. _____

22. (1) *Has* (2) *Have* either of the editorials appeared in the student newspaper?　22. _____

23. It (1) *was* (2) *were* the Finance Minister and the Governor of the Bank of Canada who convinced the Prime Minister that the country's debt was reaching critical proportions.　23. _____

24. Neither Janet nor her parents (1) *seems* (2) *seem* interested in our offer to help.　24. _____

25. He is one of those political advisers who (1) *was* (2) *were* interested in helping all Canadians to feel part of the political process.　25. _____

30. GRAMMAR: AGREEMENT—PRONOUN AND ANTECEDENT

(Study Section 27, Make Every Pronoun Agree with Its Antecedent in Person and Number.)
Write the number of the correct choice.

Example: One of the riders fell off (1) *his* (2) *their* horse.   1

1. Agatha Christie is the kind of writer who loves to keep (1) *her* (2) *their* readers guessing until the last page.   1. _____

2. Many educators advocate a national standards because (1) *we* (2) *they* hope to develop uniform expectations.   2. _____

3. If anyone has found my wallet, will (1) *he or she* (2) *they* please return it.   3. _____

4. He majored in mathematics because (1) *it* (2) *they* had always been of interest to him.   4. _____

5. She presented extensive data, though (1) *it* (2) *they* had been difficult to assemble.   5. _____

6. He assumed that every student had done (1) *his or her* (2) *their* best to complete the test.   6. _____

7. Both Eddie and David decided to stretch (1) *his* (2) *their* legs when the bus reached Kingston.   7. _____

8. Ironically, neither woman had ever lived in Cuba, the setting of (1) *her* (2) *their* novels.   8. _____

9. Each of the attorneys spent several hours outlining (1) *her* (2) *their* ideas.   9. _____

10. He buys his books at the campus bookstore because (1) *it has* (2) *they have* low prices.   10. _____

11. Neither the president nor the deans had indicated (1) *his or her* (2) *their* position.   11. _____

12. Every member of the basketball team received (1) *his or her* (2) *their* individual trophy.   12. _____

13. The class votes to have (1) *its* (2) *their* final the last day of class rather than during exam week.   13. _____

14. The jury seemed to be having difficulty in making up (1) *its mind* (2) *their minds.*   14. _____

15. Neither Aaron nor Paul has declared (1) *his* (2) *their* major.   15. _____

16. Anyone who still does not recycle (1) *his or her* (2) *their* garbage needs to read this news article.   16. _____

17. Before someone can choose a career rationally, (1) *he* (2) *they* must have sufficient information.   17. _____

18. Neither the guide nor the hikers seemed aware of (1) *her* (2) *their* danger.   18. _____

19. The faculty has already made (1) *its* (2) *their* recommendations.   19. _____

20. Critics argue that (1) *those kind* (2) *those kinds* of movies may promote violent tendencies in young people.   20. _____

21. One has to decide early in life what (1) *he or she* (2) *they* succeed at.   21. _____

22. Neither the coach nor the players underestimated (1) *his* (2) *their* opponents.   22. _____

23. Hitler and Stalin were responsible for torturing millions within (1) *his* (2) *their* own countries.   23. _____

24. Both the pilot and the copilot thought that (1) *his* (2) *their* hour had come.   24. _____

25. Neither the team nor the coach is happy about (1) *her* (2) *their* budget for the coming school year.   25. _____

26. In the next five years, owners of older vehicles polluting the environment can sell (1) *your* (2) *their* cars or trucks for scrap.   26. _____

27. If a stranger tried to talk to her, she would just look at (1) *him* (2) *them* and smile.   27. _____

28. Every one of the trees in the affected area had lost most of (1) *its* (2) *their* leaves.   28. _____

29. Some women can understand (1) *herself* (2) *themself* (3) *themselves* better through reading feminist literature.

29. _____

30. The jury seems upset about the media's determination to interview (1) *its* (2) *their* members following the verdict.

30. _____

31. A disciplinary board of both faculty and students determined that (1) *its* (2) *their* process for reviewing student complaints was too cumbersome and slow.

31. _____

32. No one should blame (1) *himself* (2) *themself* (3) *themselves* (4) *yourself* for misfortunes that cannot be prevented.

32. _____

33. Rita is one of those people who cannot control (1) *her* (2) *their* anger when under stress.

33. _____

34. Professor Brown is one of those teachers who really loves (1) *his* (2) *their* job.

34. _____

35. Everyone grabbed (1) *his* (2) *their* boots and a cafeteria tray when the heavy snowstorm hit the campus.

35. _____

36. Neither the monitors nor the resident director looked forward to how (1) *their* (2) *her* residents would react to the rodent population that had invaded the building.

36. _____

37. Each of the singers in the newly formed rap group dreamed of earning (1) *her* (2) *their* first million dollars.

37. _____

38. As part of the Kim family's Vietnamese New Year celebration, each wrote *cau doi*—which are poems about (1) *his or her* (2) *their* memories of home and family

38. _____

39. During the Christmas season, many Canadian families serve (1) *its* (2) *their* favorite dish—roast turkey with all the trimmings.

39. _____

40. If everyone would contribute a small portion of (1) *her* (2) *their* January 1 paycheck, we should be able to replace the stolen electronic equipment.

40. _____

41. Each cat claimed (1) *its* (2) *their* specific area of the bedroom for long afternoon naps.

41. _____

42. The deaf now have a telecommunication device to allow (1) *he* (2) *them* to make phone calls to a hearing person.

42. _____

43. When a grocery packer slams my food into a bag, I usually give (1) *her* (2) *them* a stern look and take over the job of packing.

43. _____

44. Everyone came to the last class to make certain (2) *him* (2) *they* understood the professor's requirements for the final.

44. _____

45. If viewers are not happy with the CBC's programming, (1) *you* (2) *they* should write letters to CRTC.

45. _____

46. Researchers have found that the type of relationship couples have can affect (1) *your* (2) *their* overall immune system.

46. _____

47. Neither the computer assistants nor the hardware specialist knows how (1) *she or he* (2) *they* should solve the current printer problem.

47. _____

48. The researchers stated that (1) *she doesn't* (2) *they don't* really understand the psychological aspect of obesity.

48. _____

49. A neighbourhood organization of young people is meeting to determine how (1) *it* (2) *they* can help elderly residents in the community.

49. _____

50. Either the lead actor or the chorus missed (1) *his* (2) *their* cue.

50. _____

31. GRAMMAR: AGREEMENT—REVIEW

(Study Section 26–27, Agreement.)

Write **1** if the sentence is **correct** in agreement.
Write **0** if it is **incorrect**.

Example: Nobody in the first two rows are singing. 0 _____

1. The deep blue of the waters seem to reflect the sky. 1. _____

2. As the highlight of the Passover holiday, all of the family participates in the Seder, which is a ceremonial feast. 2. _____

3. The current estimate of almost three million Canadians who are illiterate suggests an education system that is less than perfect. 3. _____

4. The strength of these new space-age materials have been demonstrated many times. 4. _____

5. All these experiences, along with the special love and attention that my daughter needs, have taught me the value of caring. 5. _____

6. The main reason deterring street kids from using shelters are the drug testing and rehabilitation programs. 6. _____

7. Does the six-thirty bus and the eight-o'clock train arrive in Windsor before midnight? 7. _____

8. According to a recent survey almost every person feels that their self-esteem is important. 8. _____

9. The management now turned to its last resort; they asked the federal government for help with their financial problems. 9. _____

10. When an older student senses that an institution understands nontraditional students, she generally works to her academic potential. 10. _____

11. I found that the thrill of attending university soon leaves when you have to pay your tuition. 11. _____

12. Everyone who heard the bombs declared that they had never before been so frightened. 12. _____

13. You should hire one of those experts who solves problems with computers. 13. _____

14. You should hire one of those kinds of experts who solve problems with computers. 14. _____

15. In our home, there were constant fighting and financial difficulty. 15. _____

16. Halifax or Victoria is expecting a lucrative naval contract. 16. _____

17. Bacon and eggs are no longer considered a healthy breakfast. 17. _____

18. Probably everybody in the camp except Tracey and Lisa know what happened. 18. _____

19. Neither Chuck nor Arnold are as blessed with talent as Sylvester. 19. _____

20. The management has decided that they will not sell anyone a ticket until the theatre opens its doors at noon. 20. _____

32. GRAMMAR: FRAGMENTS

(Study Section 29A, Fragments.)

Write **1** if the boldface words are a **complete sentence.**
Write **0** if they are a **fragment.**

Example: Nick was famished. *Having eaten only four hot dogs at the game* ___0___

1. *When considering the plight of the Canadian farmer.* It's also important to know that Parliament gave farmers $2 billion of direct subsidies last year. 1. _____

2. *Having applied for dozens of jobs and not having had any offers.* 2. _____

3. *The manuscript having been returned, Johanna sat down to revise it.* 3. _____

4. Harrison desperately wanted the part. *Because he believed that this was the film that would make him a star.* 4. _____

5. *Books, cameras, suitcases, blankets—all of which were piled on the porch.* 5. _____

6. He admitted to being a computer nerd. *As a matter of fact, he was proud of his personal style.* 6. _____

7. *Over 50 percent of Canadians surveyed feeling guilty about their child-care arrangements.* 7. _____

8. She parked her car. *Then she hurried into the courthouse.* 8. _____

9. Many Canadians prefer invisible taxes rather than very visible GST. *Where do you stand on this issue?* 9. _____

10. Maurice kept nodding his head as the coach explained the play. *Thinking all the time that it would never work.* 10. _____

11. *Because she was interested in rocks, she majored in geology.* 11. _____

12. I argued with two of my fellow students. *First with Edward and then with Harry.* 12. _____

13. There are many humourous research projects. *Such as developing an artificial dog to breed fleas for allergy studies.* 13. _____

14. Taylor was absolutely positive he would pass. *Regardless of having received failing grades on both his essay and the midterm.* 14. _____

15. *Colleen stepped up to the free-throw line; then she made two points to win the game.* 15. _____

16. *His term paper having been returned.* He looked eagerly for the instructor's grade. 16. _____

17. *Because he never fully realized how important a college education could be.* 17. _____

18. She went to the supermarket. *After she had made a list of groceries that she needed.* 18. _____

19. Two hours before the contest, he was very nervous. *Later, he felt very confident.* 19. _____

20. I telephoned Dr. Gross. *The man who had been our family physician for many years.* 20. _____

21. We suspect Atterley of the theft. *Because he had access to the funds and he has been living far beyond his means.* 21. _____

22. Perhaps this popular children's movie and its sequel are not so funny. *Especially when children may be tempted to create booby traps at home.* 22. _____

23. Please don't go. *Stay.* 23. _____

59

24. She is a star athlete. **Besides being a brilliant student.**   24. _____

25. I offered her a ticket to *Aida*. **An opera she had wanted to see.**   25. _____

26. Cheech Marin, currently starring in a television series, may surprise most people. **About his Iranian heritage.**

    26. _____

27. **Knowing that her time was limited, she took a taxi to the station.**   27. _____

28. **To end the controversy over what happened to the U.S. servicemen missing in action from the Vietnam War.** The United States and Vietnamese governments will have to work together to examine war archives.

    28. _____

29. Successful movie stars in the past learned. **To avoid overexposure in the media.**   29. _____

30. Roger Maris never received the credit he deserved. **Despite breaking Babe Ruth's record for home runs in a single season.**

    30. _____

31. **Although settlers began coming to Canada in the sixteenth century.** It wasn't until the nineteenth century that large groups of Europeans came to this country.

    31. _____

32. **While many Asians commemorate their ancestors and traditional community values during New Year's celebrations.**

    32. _____

33. **Listen!** It's too hot to do much yard work today without taking frequent rests in the shade.   33. _____

33. GRAMMAR: COMMA SPLICES AND FUSED SENTENCES

(Study Section 29B, Comma Splices and Fused Sentences.)

Write **1** for each item that is a **single complete sentence**.
Write **0** for each item that is a **comma splice** or **fused sentence**.

Example: The mission was a success, everyone was pleased.   0 _____

1. The critics unanimously agreed the play was terrible it closed after a week.   1. _____

2. The party broke up at midnight, Bram lingered for a few final words with Katrina.   2. _____

3. Determined to sweep the Atlantic and western provinces, the party leaders authorized extra campaign money to be spent there.   3. _____

4. If the moon enters the earth's shadow, a lunar eclipse occurs, causing the moon to turn a deep red.   4. _____

5. The ticket agent had sold eighty-one tickets to boarding passengers, yet there were only eleven empty seats on the train.   5. _____

6. Since she did not believe that humankind's destiny was determined by forces beyond its control, she insisted that people were their own greatest enemies.   6. _____

7. Sheer exhaustion having caught up with me, I had no trouble falling asleep.   7. _____

8. The restaurant check almost made me faint, because I had left my wallet home, I couldn't pay for the meal.   8. _____

9. Those of us who owned cars ignored the rule, since we were students, we never worried about campus regulations.   9. _____

10. It was a cloudy, sultry afternoon when we sighted our first school of whales, and the cry of "Lower the boats!" rang throughout the ship.   10. _____

11. The war was finally over; however, little could be done to ease the refugees' sense of loss.   11. _____

12. Author Diane Lewis describes 50 ways to recycle fruitcakes; my favourite is to use slices of fruitcake as drink coasters.   12. _____

13. The two major television networks face stiff competition for ratings, because of cable networks, viewers can have up to five hundred choices to select from as they decide what to watch.   13. _____

14. The National Archives produces *Maclean's* magazine in Braille, the library says the magazine may be requested by Members of Parliament.   14. _____

15. While Canadians are pleased about low inflation, they may not like the country's latest accomplishment, Canada leads other industrialized nations in having the highest rate on unemployment.   15. _____

16. Canadians earn less than they did ten years ago; skyrocketing housing costs are often cited as the leading cause for the decline in income.   16. _____

17. Crime in the United States suggests much about economic hardship because the majority of victims of assault crimes are male and members of ethnic or cultural minorities.   17. _____

18. As I waited in line for my turn at the automatic teller machine, I balanced my checkbook.   18. _____

19. According to a recent study, over 30 percent of Canadians from rural areas own rifles, therefore, the government must proceed carefully in drafting gun control legislation.   19. _____

20. A shortage of licensed contractors still exists in the areas hit hardest by recent floods, and homeowners have quickly learned that it's better to wait for a work crew with the proper credentials. 20. _____

21. The largest Canadian province in terms of land mass is Quebec it covers more than a million and half square kilometres, with a coast line of about ten thousand kilometres. 21. _____

22. According to some researchers, classroom educational experiences for little boys are different than those of little girls, in other words, even though it may be unintentional, teachers may have subtly different expectations based on the gender of their students. 22. _____

23. Tarantulas, which are large spiders with powerful fangs and a mean bite, live not only in the tropics but also in the southern United States. 23. _____

24. Polygraph evidence in criminal cases may not be used in a trial unless both the prosecution and the defense lawyers agree before any lie detector test is given. 24. _____

25. This particular bovine growth hormone, therefore, increases milk production in cows by almost 35 percent. 25. _____

34. GRAMMAR: FRAGMENTS, COMMA SPLICES, AND FUSED SENTENCES

(Study Section 29A, Fragments, and Section 29B, Comma Splices and Fused Sentences.)

Write **1** for each item that is a **single complete sentence.**
Write **0** for each item that is a **fragment.**

Example: A man who neither seeks out trouble nor avoids it.   0

1. Because pie, ice cream, and candy bars have practically no nutritional value.   1. _____

2. When the bindings release, the ski comes off.   2. _____

3. Which for $100,000 guarantees a moderate-sized home.   3. _____

4. Maureen McTeer and Mila Mulroney, wives of government leaders very highly publicized.   4. _____

5. Whereas older cars run on regular gas and lack complex pollution controls.   5. _____

6. That particular judicial hearing raised issues of how men and women perceive each other.   6. _____

7. If families will install and maintain smoke detectors, they may someday save family members from perishing in a fire.   7. _____

8. If nothing had come of it, her safety in the workplace being fully assured by an employee benefits contract.   8. _____

9. Which could in no way be rationally explained by any of the scientists.   9. _____

10. Wait.   10. _____

Write **1** for each item that is **one or more complete, correct sentences.**
Write **2** for each item that contains a **fragment.**
Write **3** for each item that contains a **comma splice** or **fused sentence.**

Example: Today is Monday, tomorrow is Tuesday.   3

1. Buzz Beurling was the most famous RCAF fighter pilot in the World War II, yet few Canadians now know of his past.   1. _____

2. The goalie signed the largest professional hockey contract to date; he will earn $24 million over a six-year period.   2. _____

3. Native Canadians have dances and music for every tribal ceremonial and social occasion celebrated.   3. _____

4. Scientists are currently interested in studying polar bears. Because the bears' body chemistry may reveal how pollution has affected the Arctic.   4. _____

5. Canadians, for the moment, may be slightly less concerned about their environment. Sales of environmentally friendly products have declined in the past year.   5. _____

6. The famous rock star complained bitterly to the press because she must pay her ex-husband $20,000 a month in alimony.   6. _____

7. Powwows are social events often bringing several aboriginal tribes together to celebrate a holiday, to honour tribal members, or to help raise money for a native organization, additionally, powwows offer an opportunity for native people to preserve and share their cultural history.   7. _____

8. Since 1975, over 1.5 million Vietnamese have left their homeland in search of a peaceful life, many have settled in Australia, China, Europe, the United States, and Canada.   8. _____

9. Because the founder of a popular fast-food restaurant chain has encouraged corporations to provide financial support for employees adopting children.   9. _____

10. Trolls of all shapes, sizes, and colours are back in the market, and children can't seem to get enough of them.   10. _____

11. What happened to Dunstan Ramsey and Boy Staunton is told in the novel *Fifth Business* it was written by Robertson Davies.   11. _____

12. He wore a pair of mud-encrusted, flap-soled boots they looked older than he was.   12. _____

13. He wore a pair of mud-encrusted, flap-soled boots, footgear that looked older than he was.   13. _____

14. The computer analyst produced pages of statistics, for the agency wanted to know how its money was spent.   14. _____

15. Sam reread his assignment a dozen times before handing it in. To be absolutely sure his ideas were clear.   15. _____

16. The representatives decided, however, to wait for the foreign minister's arrival before making a decision.   16. _____

17. That she is dead is beyond dispute.   17. _____

18. "I believe," declared the headmaster. "That you deserve expulsion."   18. _____

19. The scouts hiked two miles until they reached the falls, then they had lunch.   19. _____

20. The police having been warned to expect trouble, every available officer lined the avenue of the march.   20. _____

21. A still greater challenge faced them, it seemed impossible to warn the fort in time.   21. _____

22. Ireland's vital crop had been wiped out by the potato blight, nevertheless, Irish people who owned ten acres of land were disqualified from poor relief.   22. _____

23. The Irish immigrants did not go into farming for fear that the potato blight would strike again, but the German immigrants did go into farming, they had no fear of this blight.   23. _____

35. GRAMMAR: SENTENCE EFFECTIVENESS

(Study Sections 28–29, Effective Sentences.)

For each **correct** sentence, write **1.**
For each **incorrect** (ineffective) sentence, write the number that **explains** the error.

2. **failure to subordinate details**
3. **childishly choppy sentences**
4. **overuse of** *and*
5. **needless separation of subject and verb or parts of infinitive**
6. **dangling, misplaced, or squinting modifier**
7. **nonparallel structure**

8. **omission in comparison**
9. **shift in person, number, tense, voice, etc.**
10. **redundancy (including double negative and superfluous** *that*)
11. **mixed construction**
12. **inflated phrasing**

Example: He wanted *to shower* and *to sleep.*   1

Example: That was a *most unique* moment.   10

1. If one drives a car without thinking, you are more than likely to have an accident.   1. _____

2. She said that, if I helped her with her math, that she would type my paper.   2. _____

3. The entire class was so pleased at learning that Dr. Turner has rescheduled the quiz.   3. _____

4. I intended to carefully and thoughtfully consider my program for the fall term.   4. _____

5. A study revealed that vigorous exercise may add only one or two years to a person's life. This study used McGill graduates.   5. _____

6. The director, thinking only about how he could get the shot of the exploding car, endangered everyone.   6. _____

7. With her new auditory implant, Audrey heard so much better.   7. _____

8. Looking down from the top of the hill, the houses appeared to be very small.   8. _____

9. The owner of the team seems to insult her players and fans and mismanaging the finances.   9. _____

10. The witness walked into the courtroom, and then she wishes she could avoid testifying.   10. _____

11. An increase in energy taxes causes most people to consider carpooling and improving energy conservation practices in their home.   11. _____

12. The party leader carried a red book and answered endless questions regarding his policies and appeared at every press conference he could.   12. _____

13. He told me that he was going to write a letter and not to disturb him.   13. _____

14. Burt Smith is a senior citizen, and he just won national recognition for his poetry.   14. _____

15. The student selected a controversial topic for his paper, and much time was spent finding suitable sources.   15. _____

16. If a student knows how to study, he should achieve success.   16. _____

17. He went to his office. He sat down. He opened his briefcase. He read some papers.   17. _____

18. Summer is a time for parties, friendships, for athletics, and in which we can relax.   18. _____

19. Juliet and I must make a decision, within one passage of the sun across the heavens, as to whether we should be forever united in holy wedlock.

19. _____

20. The children, so happy about school being canceled because of the snowstorm, planned to ski all afternoon.

20. _____

21. I met the new Church minister in my oldest pajamas.

21. _____

22. Being a ski jumper requires nerves of steel, you have to concentrate to the utmost, and being perfectly coordinated.

22. _____

23. The situation in regard to decisions on the possible expenditure of my monetary resources is such that any commitment on my part to such expenditure must be considered with extreme caution.

23. _____

24. The plane neither had enough fuel nor proper radar equipment.

24. _____

25. My personal opinion is that I think that the Flames will win their division by ten points.

25. _____

26. The malfunctioning landing gear caused the plane to crash, killing nearly everyone on the plane; only one person survived.

26. _____

27. He couldn't hardly make himself heard because of the noise outside.

27. _____

28. The instructor wondered when did the students in the back row fall asleep.

28. _____

Write the number of the **most effective** way of expressing the given ideas.

Example: 1. At this moment in time, I regret that it was impossible for me to partake in my morning repast.
    2. I had to miss breakfast.
    3. I had not hardly enough time for breakfast.

<u> 2 </u>

1.1. There was a company in Halifax. It shortened its work week from 40 hours to 36 hours. The company's output increased.

2. A company in Halifax shortened its work week from forty hours to thirty six hours, and this company found out the company's output increased.

3. When a Halifax company shortened its work week from 40 to 36 hours, its output increased.

1. _____

2.1. Canadian theatre has been revived by a new band of actors. These new actors are from television. They find it refreshing and challenging to perform before a live audience.

2. Canadian theatre has been revived by a new breed of actors—television stars, who find it refreshing and challenging to perform before a live audience.

3. Canadian theatre has been revived by this new breed of actors, which has seen actors coming from television; they have found it refreshing and challenging to perform before a live audience.

2. _____

3.1. The terrorists revealed the condition of their hostages well after they demanded what they really wanted which was food and fuel.

2. The terrorists wanted food. They wanted the plane refueled. Until then, they didn't reveal the condition of their hostages.

3. Before revealing the condition of their hostages, the terrorists demanded fuel and food.

3. _____

4.1. The ground crew, who discovered the broken linkage Friday morning, had checked the plane Thursday night.

   2. The ground crew, who had checked the plane Thursday night, discovered the broken linkage Friday morning.

   3. The ground crew checked the plane Thursday night, and they discovered the broken linkage Friday morning.   4. _____

5.1. The papers were marked *top secret*. The term *top secret* indicates contents of extraordinary value.

   2. The papers were of extraordinary value, and, therefore, they were marked *top secret*.

   3. The papers were marked *top secret,* indicating their extraordinary value.   5. _____

36. GRAMMAR: PARALLEL STRUCTURE

(Study Section 28F, Use Parallel Structure.)

Write **1** if the boldface words or word groups are **all in parallel structure.**
Write **0** if the boldface words or word groups are **not all in parallel structure.**

Example: Lilliputian politicians practiced *leaping* and *creeping.*   1

1. Theresa impressed everyone with her *wit, charm, grace, and intelligence.*   1. _____

2. Before 8 a.m., Canada's favourite billionaire *forced five competitors into bankruptcy, lied to his mistress and sister, and then his breakfast was brought to him.*   2. _____

3. The apartment could be rented *by the week, by the month,* or *you could pay on a yearly basis.*   3. _____

4. *What I said, what I did,* and *what I endured* during those tragic days will always haunt my memory.   4. _____

5. Our new wood-burning stove *should keep us warm, save us money, and should afford us much pleasure.*   5. _____

6. Christopher Columbus has been remembered as *an entrepreneur, an explorer, and a sailor and perhaps now for how he took advantage of native populations.*   6. _____

7. My grandmother's cookbook is *old, worn,* and *has been used by three generations of women.*   7. _____

8. The chief ordered Agent 007 *to break into the building, crack the safe, and to steal the atomic yo-yo plans.*   8. _____

9. Barbara especially likes to *read Tolstoy, sketch landscapes,* and *run in marathons.*   9. _____

10. When kindergartners were asked what kind of person they wanted as teacher, they said someone who was *fair, who shares,* and *not a hitter.*   10. _____

Write **1** if the sentence **contains parallel structure.**
Write **0** if the sentence is **not parallel.**

Example: The candidate took lessons in how to kiss babies and looking honest.   0

1. I knew what I was supposed to do but not when I was supposed to do it or how I could accomplish it.   1. _____

2. The scouts marched briskly off into the woods, trekked ten miles to Cowichan Lake, and tents were erected by them.   2. _____

3. Rodney, the hero of the novel, had three main characteristics: his ambition, he hated von Stroeblicht, and his love for Maria.   3. _____

4. Grizzly bears have returned to ancestral eating and mating behaviors.   4. _____

5. Global warming may not only increase air and ocean temperatures but also to strengthen the forces causing storms.   5. _____

6. Where my father went on Friday nights, what he did there, and how much of the family's money he wasted on those occasions, I never found out until years later.   6. _____

7. The dance committee members realized that they had to either raise the ticket price or find a less expensive band. 7. _____

8. Neither regulating prices nor wages will slow inflation enough. 8. _____

9. Tightening the money supply is more effective than if taxes are raised. 9. _____

10. Charlie practiced shooting from the top of the key as well as how to dribble with either hand. 10. _____

37. GRAMMAR: PARALLEL STRUCTURE

(Study Section 28F, Use Parallel Structure.)

Write **1** if the boldface words or word groups are **all in parallel structure;** write **0** if they are not.
Then in the last three columns, identify each element as follows:

2. **noun (including gerunds)**
3. **participle**
4. **verb phrase (with or without complement)**
5. **prepositional phrase**
6. **infinitive**
7. **clause**
8. **adjective**

	Parallel 0	#1 2	#2 2	#3 4
Example: Grandmother insisted on *cleanliness, godliness, and being prompt.*	———	———	———	———
1. The job required some knowledge of *word processing, desktop publishing, and to write.* 1.	———	———	———	———
2. Jacques fought *with great skill, with epic daring, and superb intelligence.* 2.	———	———	———	———
3. The mosques of ancient Islamic Spain typically contained *ornate stone screens, long hallways, and the columns looked like spindles.* 3.	———	———	———	———
4. The castle was *built on a hill, surrounded by farmland, and commanded a magnificent view.* 4.	———	———	———	———
5. A newly discovered primate from the Amazon has *wide-set eyes, a broad nose, and the fur is striped like a zebra.* 5.	———	———	———	———
6. By nightfall, we were *tired, hungry, and grumpy.* 6.	———	———	———	———
7. The guerrillas *surrounded the village, set up their mortars, and the shelling began.* 7.	———	———	———	———
8. Sandra did not know *where she had come from, why she was there, or the time of her departure.* 8.	———	———	———	———
9. Her favourite pastimes remain *designing clothes, cooking gourmet meals, and practicing the flute.* 9.	———	———	———	———
10. Eliot's poetry is *witty, complex, and draws on his vast learning.* 10.	———	———	———	———

38. GRAMMAR: PLACEMENT OF MODIFIERS

(Study Section 29C, Needless Separation of Related Parts of a Sentence.)

Write **1** if the boldface word(s) are **correctly** placed.
Write **0** if the boldface word(s) are **incorrectly** placed.

Example: Never give a toy to a child **which can be swallowed.** _____0_____

1. He ordered a pizza for his friends **covered with pepperoni.** 1. _____

2. She had enough money to buy **only** two of the three books that she needed. 2. _____

3. Canadians **who consider medical treatment everyone's right** are debating the ethics of setting up private clinics. 3. _____

4. We knew that to **quickly and thoroughly** cleanse the wound was necessary. 4. _____

5. We saw the plane taxi onto the field **that would soon be leaving for Toronto.** 5. _____

6. Unfortunately, many Canadians are spending **almost** a third of their income on rent. 6. _____

7. Derek found a clue in his bedroom **that he had never seen before.** 7. _____

8. The newspaper advertised **damaged** men's suits. 8. _____

9. We hurriedly bought a picnic table from a clerk **with collapsible legs.** 9. _____

10. We learned that no one could discard anything at the municipal dump **except people living in the community.** 10. _____

11. We had trouble finding a **red, white, and blue** child's violin for the show. 11. _____

12. Although he has tried several times, he just can't learn to drive a car **with a standard shift.** 12. _____

13. The bride walked down the aisle with her father **wearing her mother's wedding gown.** 13. _____

14. Despite her sincerity and honesty, the candidate failed to **completely** explain why she dropped out of the campaign. 14. _____

15. "This is the best book I **almost** ever read!" she exclaimed. 15. _____

16. Call, **after you have addressed these 106 envelopes,** me at home. 16. _____

17. **Only** one teacher seems able to convince Raymond that he should study. 17. _____

18. Only a few Canadian Olympic athletes can expect lucrative endorsement contracts **with gold medals.** 18. _____

19. We watched the _Queen Elizabeth II_ as she slowly sailed out to sea **from our hotel window.** 19. _____

20. Indicate **on the enclosed sheet** whether you are going to the class picnic. 20. _____

21. A **battered** man's hat was hanging on a branch of the tree. 21. _____

22. This fall, television shows have been criticized for stereotyping middle-class men **on commercial networks.** 22. _____

23. Olympic swimmers often shave off their body hair **that are intent on winning their races.** 23. _____

24. Ian Greenstone said **when he realized that his grandmother was moving in with his family** that many households are now multigenerational. 24. _____

25. He replied **usually** they went to Paris in the spring. 25. _____

39. GRAMMAR: DANGLING MODIFIERS

(Study Section 29D, Dangling Modifiers.)

Write **1** if the boldface words are used **correctly**.
Write **0** if they are used **incorrectly** (dangling).

Example: *Dancing to stardom,* fame is elusive goal.   0

1. *Announcing his first hockey game in 1952,* the late Danny Gallivan began a broadcasting career that would last for over thirty years.   1. _____

2. *Rowing across the lake,* the moon often disappeared behind the clouds.   2. _____

3. *Having walked three miles,* the cabin was a welcome sight for all of us.   3. _____

4. *While shaving,* the idea for a new play came to him.   4. _____

5. *Trapped alone there at midnight,* the house creaked and moaned with every step.   5. _____

6. *Upon entering college,* he applied for part-time employment in the library.   6. _____

7. *Practicing every day for five hours,* Dani's expensive music lessons really paid off.   7. _____

8. *Sleeping in late,* the house seemed incredibly quiet with the boys still in bed.   8. _____

9. *After waiting for an hour,* word reached us that the speaker had been delayed.   9. _____

10. *When nine years old,* my father took my sister and me on our first camping trip.   10. _____

11. *At the age of ten,* I was permitted to go, for the first time, to a summer camp.   11. _____

12. *After putting away my fishing equipment,* the surface of the lake became choppy.   12. _____

13. *Racing toward the primate section of the zoo,* the chimpanzees' playful laughter drew the children to their cage.   13. _____

14. *To achieve a goal,* a person must expect to work and to make sacrifices.   14. _____

15. *Suggesting that the Canadian standard of living has declined,* many Canadian economists predict a gloomy financial status for the next generation.   15. _____

16. *After hearing of Tom's need for financial aid,* a hundred dollars was put at his disposal.   16. _____

17. *Pickled in spiced vinegar,* the host thought the peaches would go with the meat.   17. _____

18. *While protecting herself against assault,* the gun slipped from her grasp.   18. _____

19. *Disappointed at the poor attendance,* the play closed Saturday night.   19. _____

20. *Discovering that I had left my wallet at home,* I asked Janet to pay for our lunch.   20. _____

21. *As a teenager,* Darlene worked two jobs to help her family financially.   21. _____

22. *Eating too much chocolate,* my scale revealed that I had gained ten pounds.   22. _____

23. Finally, *after working for days,* the garden was free of weeds.   23. _____

24. *To receive a reply to your questions,* a self-addressed envelope is needed.   24. _____

25. *After finishing my assignment,* the dog ate it.   25. _____

40. GRAMMAR: DANGLING MODIFIERS

(Study Section 29D, Dangling Modifiers.)

Write **1** if the boldface words are used **correctly.**
Write **0** if the boldface words are used **incorrectly.**
In the second column, write the word to which the boldface words now refer.

Example: *After dancing the lead in* **Swan Lake,** cheers filled the hall.   0   a dancer

1. *Writing during the Renaissance,* poems were characterized as speaking pictures.   1. ___ _____

2. *Approaching New York,* the view of the Manhattan skyline was exciting.   2. ___ _____

3. *To have a just society,* discrimination in all forms must disappear.   3. ___ _____

4. *After searching for two weeks,* my red leather glove turned up in the yard under a melting snow bank.   4. ___ _____

5. *Realizing the unemployment rate is still over 10 percent,* most workers are not changing jobs.   5. ___ _____

6. *Having triumphed in Word War II,* many Canadians felt the Twentieth Century really did belong to Canada.   6. ___ _____

7. *Considering itself morally bound to act as peace keeper,* Canada participates in UN missions all over the world.   7. ___ _____

8. *To get a passing grade in this course,* the professor's little quirks must be considered.   8. ___ _____

9. *Sleeping until noon each day,* the sunlight shining through the window wouldn't wake me.   9. ___ _____

10. *Having read the morning paper,* it was tossed aside.   10. ___ _____

41. GRAMMAR: REVIEW

(Study Section 1–29, Grammar.)

Write **1** for each statement that is **true**.
Write **0** for each that is **false**.

Example: A *present participle* is a word that ends in *-ing* and is used as an adjective.   __1__

1. Both a **gerund** and a **present participle** end in -ing.   1. _____
2. The greatest number of words ever used in a **verb** is four.   2. _____
3. **Parallel structure** is used to designate ideas that are not equal in importance.   3. _____
4. **A dangling participle** may be corrected by being changed into a dependent clause.   4. _____
5. *It's* is a **contraction** of *it is; its* is the **possessive form** of the pronoun *it*.   5. _____
6. The **predicate precedes the subject** in a sentence beginning with the expletive *there*.   6. _____
7. A **preposition** may contain two or more words; *because of* is an example.   7. _____
8. The **principal parts of a verb** are the present tense, the future tense, and the past participle. 8. _____
9. A **collective noun** may be followed by either a singular or plural verb.   9. _____
10. A **prepositional phrase** may be used only as an adjective modifier.   10. _____
11. A **compound sentence** is one that contains two or more independent clauses.   11. _____
12. Not all **adverbs** end in *-ly*.   12. _____
13. *To lie* is an **intransitive verb**; *to lay* is a **transitive verb** and is always followed by a direct object. 13. _____
14. A **noun clause** may be introduced by the subordinate conjunction *although*.   14. _____
15. An **adjective clause** may begin with *when* or *where*.   15. _____
16. Both **verbals** and **verbs** may have modifiers and complements.   16. _____
17. The terminal punctuation of a declarative sentence is the **exclamation point.**   17. _____
18. *Without* is a **subordinate conjunction.**   18. _____
19. A sentence beginning with *because* must have both a **dependent** and an **independent clause.** 19. _____
20. The **predicate** of a sentence cannot consist of merely a past participle.   20. _____
21. A **subjective complement** may be a noun, a pronoun, or an adverb.   21. _____
22. A **direct object** may be a noun or a pronoun.   22. _____
23. An **indirect object** always follows a direct object.   23. _____
24. An **objective complement** always precedes the direct object.   24. _____
25. The words *to be* or *to have been*, when preceded by a noun or pronoun, are followed by an **object pronoun.**   25. _____
26. The word *scissors* takes a **singular verb.**   26. _____
27. An **antecedent** is the noun for which a pronoun stands.   27. _____
28. A **simple sentence** contains two or more independent clauses.   28. _____

29. Pronouns in the **objective case** always follow forms of the verb *to be.*   29. _____

30. Joining two independent clauses with only the comma (a **comma splice**) is considered incorrect.   30. _____

31. A **sentence fragment** is not considered a legitimate unit of expression; a **nonsentence** is.   31. _____

32. **Adjectives** never stand next to the words they modify.   32. _____

33. Not all words ending in *-ly* are **adverbs.**   33. _____

34. An **indefinite pronoun** designates no particular person.   34. _____

35. The words *have* and *has* identify the **present perfect tense** of a verb.   35. _____

36. An **absolute phrase** consists essentially of a noun or a pronoun and a participle.   36. _____

37. An **adverb** may modify a noun, an adjective, or another adverb.   37. _____

38. **Verbs** are words that assert an action or a state of being.   38. _____

39. The **indicative mood** of a verb is used to express a command or a request.   39. _____

40. The function of a **subordinate conjunction** is to join a dependent clause to a main clause.   40. _____

41. A **predicate** need not agree in number with its subject.   41. _____

42. An **adjective** may modify a noun, a pronoun, or an adverb.   42. _____

43. A **gerund** is a word ending in *-ing* and used as a noun.   43. _____

44. A **clause** differs from a **phrase** in that a clause always has a subject and a predicate.   44. _____

45. **Adjectives** tell what kind, how many, or which one; **adverbs** tell when, where, how, and to what degree.   45. _____

46. **Pronouns ending in *-self*** (*himself, myself*, etc.) should not be substituted for **personal pronouns** (*he, me*, etc.)   46. _____

47. **Coordinate conjunctions** (*and, but, or, nor, for, yet*) join words, phrases, and clauses of equal importance.   47. _____

48. **Pronouns in the objective case** (*him, me*, etc.) should be used as direct objects of verbs and verbals.   48. _____

49. A **linking verb** agrees with its subjective complement.   49. _____

50. When a **subject** that is singular is joined by *or* to another that is plural, the verb agrees with the farther subject.   50. _____

Write **1** if the sentence is **correct.**
Write **0** if it is **incorrect.**

Example: Was that letter sent to Paul or **I?**	0
1. **Having been notified to come at once,** there was no opportunity for me to call you.	1. _____
2. I suspected that his remarks were directed to Larry and **me.**	2. _____
3. He, **thinking that he might find his friends on the second floor of the library,** hurried.	3. _____
4. She refused to drive in that area **without** I going with her.	4. _____
5. In the cabin of the boat **was** a radio, a set of flares, and a map of the area.	5. _____
6. The Queen, standing beside her husband, children, and grandchildren, **were** waving regally at the crowd.	6. _____
7. She is a person **who** I think is certain to succeed as a social worker.	7. _____

8. **Is** there any other questions you wish to ask regarding the assignment?   8. _____

9. **Do** either of you know the purpose of this unscheduled meeting?   9. _____

10. He particularly enjoys **water skiing** and **to paddle** a canoe.   10. _____

11. Forward the complaint to **whoever** you think is in charge.   11. _____

12. Every girl and boy **was** to have an opportunity to try out for the soccer team.   12. _____

13. Neither the bus driver nor the passengers **were** aware of their danger.   13. _____

14. Families in the 1940s often lived **not only** without electricity **but also** with only outdoor bathroom facilities.   14. _____

15. Not everyone feels that **their** life is better since the abolition of the death penalty.   15. _____

16. Homemade bread tastes **differently** from bakery bread.   16. _____

17. **Not having had the chance to consult his lawyer,** it was impossible for him to remember his mother's name.   17. _____

18. **Is either of your friends** interested in watching a television program with me?   18. _____

19. He enrolled in economics because **it** had always been of interest to him.   19. _____

20. Jacob read **steady** for two weeks before he finished his novel.   20. _____

21. Burt paced nervously up and down the corridor. **Because Howard had never been this late before.**   21. _____

22. **A heavy rain began without warning,** the crew struggled with the tarpaulin.   22. _____

23. To have better control over spending, **the checkbook is balanced each week.**   23. _____

24. The Babe asked for time, stepped out of the batter's box, **and his finger was pointed toward the bleachers.**   24. _____

25. The jury could not make up **its** mind about Roderick's guilt.   25. _____

42. PUNCTUATION: THE COMMA

(Study Sections 30–32, The Comma.)

If **no comma** is needed in the bracketed space(s), write **0** in the blank at the right.
If **one or more commas** are needed, write in the blank the number (**1** to **10** from the list below) of the **reason** for the comma(s). (Use only one number in each blank.)

1. **independent clauses joined by** *and, but, or, nor, for, yet*
2. **introductory adverb clause**
3. **series**
4. **parenthetical expression (other than nonrestrictive clause)**
5. **nonrestrictive clause**

6. **appositive**
7. **absolute phrase**
8. **direct address**
9. **mild interjection**
10. **direct quotation**

Example: Donald's nephews are Huey[ ] Dewey[ ] and Louie.   3

1. *The Mysterious Assaults From Hell* [ ] a book by Deodat Lawson[ ] narrates what the author observed at 1692 Salem witch trials.   1. _____

2. Professors[ ] who assign long papers[ ] may have small classes.   2. _____

3. Well[ ] I guess we'll have to leave without Judith.   3. _____

4. If there are no other questions[ ] let's begin our game.   4. _____

5. So you see[ ] Mr. Holmes [ ] the red–headed woman couldn't possibly be the murderer.   5. _____

6. Phillip's father[ ] who is a conservative gentleman[ ] disapproves of teenage antics.   6. _____

7. Brian and Mila[ ] however[ ] hope he'll still receive a United Nations appointment.   7. _____

8. John Fitzgerald Kennedy[ ] the thirty-fifth President of the United States[ ] was assassinated on November 22, 1963.   8. _____

9. Instead of talking about yourself, listen to others[ ] for you'll be viewed as an excellent conversationalist.   9. _____

10. Before you meet clients for the first time[ ] learn all that you can about their company, their style, and their risk-taking ability.   10. _____

11. He sat down at his desk last evening[ ] and made a preliminary draft of his speech.   11. _____

12. Julie went into the library[ ] but she hurried out a few minutes later.   12. _____

13. Manning spoke angrily about needless government spending[ ] extravagant MP's pensions[ ] and quickly rising taxes.   13. _____

14. After she had watched her favourite television program[ ] she settled down to study.   14. _____

15. The candidate gave a number of speeches in St. John[ ] where she hoped to win support.   15. _____

16. She has always wanted to visit the small village[ ] where her father had lived.   16. _____

17. My instructor[ ] Prof. Ursula Franklin [ ] outlined the work for the current semester.   17. _____

18. What you need[ ] David[ ] is a professional organizer to straighten out your office.   18. _____

19. "Is this[ ]" she asked[ ] "the only excuse that you have to offer?"   19. _____

20. Eighty-four percent of all people who have AIDS in this country[ ] according to medical statistics[ ] are between 20 and 49 years old and are currently employed.   20. _____

21. His hands swollen from five ant bites[ ] John swore that he would rid his yard of all ant hills.   21. _____

22. Yes[ ] the meeting will last longer than we originally planned.   22. _____

23. Joyce became a doctor[ ] and Claude became a laboratory technician.   23. _____

24. We were asked to read *A Jest of God* [ ] which is a novel by Margaret Laurence.   24. _____

25. Sir John A. MacDonald[ ] Canada's first prime minister [ ] died in 1891.   25. _____

43. PUNCTUATION: THE COMMA

(Study Sections 30–32, The Comma.)

If no comma is needed in the bracketed space(s), write **0** in the blank at the right.
If one or more commas are needed, write in the blank the number (**1** to **10** from the list below) of the **reason** for the comma(s). (Use only one number in each blank.)

1. **parenthetical expression**   6. **contrast**
2. **nonrestrictive clause**   7. **omission**
3. **direct address**   8. **confirmatory question**
4. **after** *yes* **and** *no*   9. **date**
5. **before** *such as, especially,* **or** *particularly*   10. **state or country**

Example: The Allies invaded Normandy on June 6[ ] 1944.   9

1. Our house[ ] which had stood since 1901[ ] burned to the ground.   1. _____

2. Prime Minister [ ] would you comment on reports that you will not run again?   2. _____

3. Halifax[ ] Nova Scotia[ ] was the site of the explosion.   3. _____

4. Seashells are an exquisite natural sculpture[ ] aren't they?   4. _____

5. You will agree[ ] of course[ ] with the board's decision.   5. _____

6. I hope[ ] Charles and Mary[ ] that you will come to see us often.   6. _____

7. The person[ ] who did that to you[ ] should go to prison.   7. _____

8. For this production, John played Robert; Judith[ ] Harriet.   8. _____

9. Is it true[ ] sir[ ] that you are unwilling to be interviewed by the press?   9. _____

10. Our next contestant comes all the way from Don Mills[ ] Ontario[ ] just to be with us today.   10. _____

11. Frank graduated from the University of Victoria; Esther[ ] from McGill University.   11. _____

12. Students[ ] who work their way through college[ ] learn to value their college years.   12. _____

13. She said, "No[ ] I absolutely refuse to answer your question."   13. _____

14. The geography of Latin America is marked with many types of terrain[ ] such as lowlands, rain
    forests, vast plains, high plateaus, and fertile valleys.   14. _____

15. On October 11[ ] 1985[ ] our adopted son arrived from Korea.   15. _____

16. The film had been advertised as a children's movie[ ] not a production full of violence.   16. _____

17. Nevertheless[ ] we were fortunate to have recovered of our luggage.   17. _____

18. The instructor told us to read the poem[ ] and to write our impressions of it.   18. _____

19. You are expecting to spend the evening with us[ ] aren't you?   19. _____

20. I've already told you[ ] little boy[ ] that I'm not giving back your ball.   20. _____

21. Gweneth Lloyd[ ] who won the 1992 Governor General's Performing Arts Award[ ] created her
    most famous piece in 1942, entitled *The Wise Virgins*.   21. _____

22. Not everyone[ ] who objected to the new ruling[ ] signed the petition.   22. _____

23. It was[ ] on the other hand[ ] an opportunity that he could not turn down.   23. _____

24. Brian Mulroney[ ] who led the government for nine years[ ] introduced the GST in 1991.   24. _____

25. She has several hobbies[ ] such as collecting coins writing verse, and growing roses.   25. _____

44. PUNCTUATION: THE COMMA

(Study Sections 30–32, The Comma.)

If no comma is needed in the bracketed space(s), write **0** in the blank at the right.
If one or more commas are needed, write in the blank the number (**1 to 11** from the list below) of the **reason** for the comma(s).
(Use only one number in each blank.)

1. **independent clauses joined by** *and, but, for, or, nor, so, yet*
2. **introductory adverb clause**
3. **long introductory prepositional phrase**
4. **introductory participial phrase**
5. **introductory infinitive phrase**
6. **series**

7. **coordinate adjectives**
8. **appositive**
9. **absolute phrase**
10. **mild interjection**
11. **direct quotation**

Example: James Joyce[ ] Ireland's most famous novelist[ ] lived most of his life abroad.   ___8___

1. The Hamilton Ti–Cats have good running backs[ ] and look good on defense as well.   1. _____

2. Well[ ] we'll probably see another foot of snow before the winter ends.   2. _____

3. Agatha Christie[ ] the famous mystery writer[ ] caricatured herself in her books.   3. _____

4. Convinced of her client's innocence[ ] the young lawyer searched for additional reliable witnesses.   4. _____

5. The concert having ended[ ] the fans rushed toward the stage.   5. _____

6. He hoped to write short stories[ ] publish his poems[ ] and plan a novel.   6. _____

7. If parents wish to send their children to boarding school[ ] they should find one with a small student-to-staff ratio.   7. _____

8. Many people had tried to reach the top of the mountain[ ] but only a few had succeeded.   8. _____

9. Equipped with only an inexpensive camera[ ] she succeeded in taking a prize-winning picture.   9. _____

10. During times of emotional distress and heightened tensions[ ] Madeline remains calm.   10. _____

11. To cure alcoholism in the 1840s[ ] physicians often prescribed opium for their patients.   11. _____

12. Recognizing that his position was hopeless[ ] Krilov resigned.   12. _____

13. Physicians didn't understand alcoholism[ ] and they underestimated the addictive qualities of opium.   13. _____

14. Mr. Novak found himself surrounded by noisy[ ] exuberant students.   14. _____

15. "We are[ ]" she said[ ] "prepared to serve meals to a group of considerable size."   15. _____

16. Carol had no intention of withdrawing from college[ ] nor was she willing to carry a lighter program.   16. _____

17. To improve a child's diet[ ] add more beans and green vegetables to the meals.   17. _____

18. Although storm clouds were gathering[ ] we made the trip across the lake in the canoe.   18. _____

19. "You must be more quiet[ ] or the landlord will make us move," she said.   19. _____

20. We asked Pat Barton[ ] the Cub Scout director[ ] to suggest a suitable campsite.   20. _____

21. I could not decide whether to attend to college[ ] or to travel to Nigeria with my aunt. 21. _____

22. Built on a high cliff[ ] the house afforded a panoramic view of the valley below. 22. _____

23. Our phone constantly ringing[ ] we decided to rely on the answering machine to avoid interruptions during supper. 23. _____

24. The professor raised his voice to a low roar[ ] the class having apparently dozed off. 24. _____

25. Her courses include Russian[ ] organic chemistry[ ] and marine biology. 25. _____

45. PUNCTUATION: THE COMMA

(Study Sections 30–32, The Comma.)
In the blank,

write **1** if the punctuation in brackets is **correct;**
write **0** if it is **incorrect.**

(Use only one number in each blank.)

Example: We would appreciate it[,] therefore[,] if you paid our bill and left.   <u> 1 </u>

1. She died[,] because she had been unable to find shelter.   1. _____

2. We traveled to Manitoba[,] and went down the Red River.   2. _____

3. "Tell me," he demanded[,] "who you are."   3. _____

4. When the results were in[,] Stewart was the winner.   4. _____

5. You expect to graduate in June[,] don't you?   5. _____

6. O'Conner started the second half at linebacker[,] O'Hara having torn his knee ligaments.   6. _____

7. O'Conner started the second half at linebacker[,] O'Hara had torn his knee ligaments.   7. _____

8. Trying to concentrate[,] Susan closed the door and turned off the television set.   8. _____

9. "My fellow Canadians[,] I look forward to the opportunity to serve this country," he said.   9. _____

10. Some of the older and more conservative members of the tennis club[,] did not approve of Roseanne's dress.   10. _____

11. Judy, who especially enjoys baseball, sat in the front row[,] and watched the game closely.   11. _____

12. "Are you going to a fire?"[,] the police officer asked the speeding motorist.   12. _____

13. Two of the students left the office[,] the third waited to see the dean.   13. _____

14. The coach and three of her players[,] recently appeared on a television program.   14. _____

15. "I won't wait any longer," she said[,] picking up her books from the bench.   15. _____

16. The rugged[,] snow-covered mountains inspired the poet to write about nature.   16. _____

17. The relatively short drought[,] nonetheless[,] had still caused much damage to the crops.   17. _____

18. The apartment they rented[,] had neither screens nor storm windows.   18. _____

19. According to the polls, the candidate was losing[,] he blamed the media for the results.   19. _____

20. However[,] much you may think you like ice cream, two litres will be too much.   20. _____

21. In Sayward, British Columbia[,] in November 1990, many people lost their homes because of severe flooding.   21. _____

22. "Did you know," the TV pitch man warned[,] "that each year thousands of prizes go unclaimed?"   22. _____

23. Her grandfather[,] who has trouble understanding young people today[,] frowned and left the room.   23. _____

24. Irving Layton[,] the author of many books of poetry[,] has a degree in agriculture.   24. _____

25. Next summer, she hopes to fulfill a lifelong wish[,] to travel to the Queen Charlotte Islands.   25. _____

26. First-graders now engage in writing journals[,] in problem-solving activities[,] and in brief science experiments; they definitely do more than memorize the alphabet.   26. _____

27. Her last day in the office[,] was spent in sorting papers and filing manuscripts.   27. _____

28. In preparation for their retirement[,] many Canadians begin saving as soon as they find a full-time position.   28. _____

29. Having loaded her word processor[,] Baharti's quest for the perfect Harlequin romance began.   29. _____

30. Haven't you any idea[,] of the responsibility involved in running a household?   30. _____

31. Even though Levi Strauss began by making denim tents[,] he soon switched to making pants for cowboys.   31. _____

32. Shaking hands with his patient, the physician asked[,] "Now what kind of surgery are we doing today?"   32. _____

33. Great balls of fire[,] the cat is in the hamster cage again!   33. _____

34. May and Judy were determined to find a less painful[,] but effective diet.   34. _____

35. A cowboy's hat actually had many purposes besides shielding his face from the sun and rain[,] for many cowboys used their hats as a pillow and a drinking cup.   35. _____

36. During conversations about controversial topics[,] our faces communicate a lot of information, especially our emotional responses.   36. _____

37. John Diefenbaker[,] a skilled and polished speaker[,] effectively used town meetings during his many years in public life.   37. _____

38. To understand how different types of living arrangements impact student relationships[,] the psychology department completed several informal observational studies on campus.   38. _____

39. Over the centuries, in many parts of Africa, people have organized themselves according to class[,] and not tribes.   39. _____

40. The provinces with the largest number of dairy cows are Quebec[,] Ontario[,] and British Columbia.   40. _____

41. Young Soo's mother was preparing *kimchi*[,] a pickled cabbage dish that is commonly eaten with Korean meals.   41. _____

42. Establishing and maintaining friendships must be an important aspect of our culture[,] for many popular television series focus on how a group of characters care for their friendships with one another.   42. _____

43. Researchers have discovered that people beginning an intimate relationship use a significant number of affectionate expressions[,] but the frequency of these expressions drop as the relationship matures.   43. _____

44. Working hard to pay the mortgage, to educate their children, and to save money for retirement[,] many of Canada's middle class now call themselves the "new poor."   44. _____

45. The children could take martial arts classes near home[,] or they could decide to save their money for summer camp.   45. _____

46. Canadian families have changed over the last fifty years; now only 68 percent of children live with both biological parents[,] 20 percent of children live in single-parent families[,] and 9 percent live with one biological parent and a stepparent.   46. _____

47. David was hungry for a gooey[,] chocolate brownie smothered in whipped cream and chocolate sauce.   47. _____

48. His thoughts overwhelmed with grief[,] Jack decided to postpone his vacation for another month.   48. _____

49. "Oh[,] I forgot to bring my report home to finish it tonight," sighed Mary.   49. _____

50. People exercise because it makes them feel good[,] they may even become addicted to exercise.   50. _____

46. PUNCTUATION: THE COMMA

(Study Sections 30–32, The Comma.)

If there should be **a comma** at any one or more of the numbered spaces in a sentence, circle the corresponding number(s) in the column at the right.
If there should be **no commas** in the sentence, circle **0**.

Example: I'll have a hamburger$_1$ fries$_2$ and a coke$_3$ with lots of$_4$ ice.　　　　0 ①② 3 4

1. College students$_1$ need a good dictionary$_2$ a desk$_3$ and some patience and enthusiasm$_4$ to

   succeed in their first composition class.　　　　1. 0 1 2 3 4

2. Because of the dramatic increase$_1$ in home insurance premiums in Canada$_2$ many Canadians

   have not been able$_3$ to afford complete coverage$_4$.　　　　2. 0 1 2 3 4

3. Under the proposed$_1$ unemployment insurance reforms$_2$ companies$_3$ in industries where layoffs

   are common will have to pay$_4$ higher premiums.　　　　3. 0 1 2 3 4

4. Women$_1$ will you$_2$ allow more movies$_3$ depicting violence against your sisters$_4$ to be

   produced?　　　　4. 0 1 2 3 4

5. I wanted$_1$ to go$_2$ to McMaster; Terry$_3$ to Acadia.　　　　5. 0 1 2 3

6. No$_1$ I know nothing$_2$ regarding$_3$ her whereabouts.　　　　6. 0 1 2 3

7. I phoned Jack$_1$ this morning$_2$ but$_3$ he wasn't at home.　　　　7. 0 1 2 3

8. The MP$_1$ who had already served two years as Minister of Finance$_2$ and one as Minister of

   Justice$_3$ resigned his seat.　　　　8. 0 1 2 3

9. Emily was born on July 21$_1$ 1987$_2$ in Montreal$_3$ Quebec$_4$ during a thunderstorm.　　　　9. 0 1 2 3 4

10. I consider him$_1$ to be$_2$ a hard-working student$_3$ but$_4$ I may be wrong.　　　　10. 0 1 2 3 4

11. Audrey$_1$ a woman$_2$ whom I met last summer$_3$ is here$_4$ to see me.　　　　11. 0 1 2 3 4

12. Having an interest$_1$ in anthropology$_2$ she frequently audited$_3$ Dr. Irwin's class$_4$ that met on

    Saturdays.　　　　12. 0 1 2 3 4

13. Her friends$_1$ her relatives$_2$ and her husband$_3$ urged her to reconsider her decision$_4$ to leave.　　　　13. 0 1 2 3 4

14. Well$_1$ I dislike her intensely$_2$ but$_3$ she is quite clever$_4$ to be sure.　　　　14. 0 1 2 3 4

15. To solve$_1$ her legal problems$_2$ she consulted an attorney$_3$ whom she knew$_4$ from college.　　　　15. 0 1 2 3 4

16. "To what"$_1$ he asked$_2$ "do you attribute$_3$ your great popularity$_4$ with the students?" 16. 0 1 2 3 4

17. Some of the specimens$_1$ that you will see on display today$_2$ were alive more than 100,000 years ago$_3$ when the dinosaurs were masters$_4$ of the earth. 17. 0 1 2 3 4

18. "Blowing in the Wind"$_1$ a folk song written by Bob Dylan$_2$ in 1962$_3$ promises$_4$ that life will get better through time. 18. 0 1 2 3 4

19. Many filmmakers are creating$_1$ serious movies$_2$ about their cultural heritage; however$_3$ there are few$_4$ commercially successful Canadian movies about Chinese or Black cultures. 19. 0 1 2 3 4

20. "You haven't seen my glasses$_1$ have you?" Granny asked$_2$ the twins$_3$ thinking they had hidden them$_4$ somewhere in the den. 20. 0 1 2 3 4

21. The car having broken down$_1$ because of a dirty carburetor$_2$ we missed the first act$_3$ in which$_4$ Hamlet confronts his father's ghost. 21. 0 1 2 3 4

22. After she had paid her tuition$_1$ she checked in at the residence hall$_2$ that she had chosen$_3$ and soon began$_4$ unloading her suitcases and boxes. 22. 0 1 2 3 4

23. The day was so warm$_1$ and sunny$_2$ that the entire class wished fervently$_3$ that the lecture would take place$_4$ outdoors. 23. 0 1 2 3 4

24. Daniel Day-Lewis$_1$ who won an Oscar for the movie *My Left Foot*$_2$ starred$_3$ in a quite different film$_4$ *The Last of the Mohicans*. 24. 0 1 2 3 4

25. The road to Lennoxville$_1$ being coated with ice$_2$ we proceeded$_3$ slowly$_4$ and cautiously. 25. 0 1 2 3 4

47. PUNCTUATION: THE COMMA

(Study Sections 30–32, The Comma.)

The following sentences **either** need a comma **or** contain an incorrectly used comma. In the first column, write the word **after** which a comma needs to be placed **or after** which comma needs to be removed.
In the second column, select a reason for making your correction from the list below.
The sentence needs a comma because there is (are)

1. **two independent clauses joined by** *and, but, for, or, nor, so, yet*
2. **an introductory adverb clause**
3. **an introductory phrase (long prepositional, participle, infinitive, or absolute)**
4. **a series**
5. **an appositive**
6. **a nonrestrictive clause or phrase**

The comma that is there now is wrong because

7. **There is no full clause after the conjunction.**
8. **The comma separates the subject from its verb.**
9. **The comma separates the verb from its complement.**
10. **There is a restrictive (or essential) clause.**

Example: When Frank and Joe looked around the stranger had vanished.   around   2

Example: The sun, shone brightly.   sun   8

1. There was much to do before her guests arrived for dinner but Betty did not know where to begin.   1. _____ ___

2. That it is indeed time for extremely serious commitment and concerted action on your part, is evident.   2. _____ ___

3. Having examined and reexamined the ancient manuscript the committee of scholars declared it genuine.   3. _____ ___

4. If Professor Routman can convince the board that she is right, the curriculum will include Chaucer's major poems, and Shakespeare's major tragedies.   4. _____ ___

5. Michael has ambitious plans to finish his novel, start a play and work on his dissertation.   5. _____ ___

6. Many Canadians prefer documentary films on television, that present in-depth coverage.   6. _____ ___

7. The country, that receives the most media attention often is the recipient of the most aid from the United Nations.   7. _____ ___

8. Housing programs use a screening process, and security procedures have actually worked well.   8. _____ ___

9. George and Robert thoroughly and painstakingly considered, what had to be done to defuse the bomb.   9. _____ ___

10. If ever there were the law on one side, and simple justice on the other, here is such a situation.   10. _____ ___

11. Peter Gzowski, host of Canada's most popular radio program wrote *The Morningside Papers* to convey a sample of the letters and poems he receives from listeners.

11. _____ ___

12. Emily Carr, will be remembered as a painter of West Coast Indians and nature.

12. _____ ___

13. Claiming that he was just offering good advice Ace frequently would tell me which card to play.

13. _____ ___

14. What gave Helen the inspiration for her short story, was her mother's account of growing up on a farm.

14. _____ ___

15. Owen's baseball cards included such famous examples as Willie Mays's running catch in the 1954 World Series, and Hank Aaron's record-breaking home run.

15. _____ ___

16. The volume that was the most valuable in the library's rare book collection, was a First Folio edition of Shakespeare's plays.

16. _____ ___

17. A film enjoyed by millions of people throughout the world *Gone with the Wind* was first thought unlikely to be a commercial success.

17. _____ ___

18. With many men feeling dissatisfied with dance aerobics a new type of exercise has quickly become popular—boxing aerobics.

18. _____ ___

19. Expo outfielder Larry Walker had 127 hits, and batted in 78 runs during the strike–shortened 1994 season.

19. _____ ___

20. The criminal mind Jessica thought to herself, is even craftier than I had imagined.

20. _____ ___

48. PUNCTUATION: THE PERIOD, QUESTION MARK, AND EXCLAMATION POINT

(Study Sections 33–34, The Period; Sections 35–36, The Question Mark; and Sections 37–38, The Exclamation Point.)

Write **1** if the punctuation inside the brackets is **correct.**
Write **0** if it is **incorrect.**

(Use only one number in each blank.)

Example: Are we having fun yet [?]   1. __1__

1. You'd like that, wouldn't you [?]   1. _____

2. "Evacuate the hall; there's a fire!" the chief shouted [!]   2. _____

3. The police officer calmly inquired if I had the slightest notion of just how fast I was backing up [?]   3. _____

4. Mr. Hall and Miss [.] James will chair the committee.   4. _____

5. The chem [.] test promises to be challenging.   5. _____

6. A Rolex watch, a diamond pendant, an emerald ring, etc. [,] were just a few of the things Maria
    wanted for her birthday.   6. _____

7. Good afternoon, ma'am [.] May I present you with a free scrub brush?   7. _____

8. The writer asked [?] "Will there be professional baseball in the spring if team owners and players
    can't resolve contract disputes?"   8. _____

9. His next question—wouldn't you know [?]—was, "What do you need, ma'am?"   9. _____

10. The professor asked, "Is it too much to ask `How prepared are you for the final?'[?]"   10. _____

11. "What a magnificent view you have of the mountains [!]" said he.   11. _____

12. Who said, "If at first you don't succeed, try, try again"[?]   12. _____

13. The man on the street corner told me that the special sale price of the watch would be $25 [.] for
    just another ten minutes.   13. _____

14. HELP WANTED: Executive sec'y [.] with min. 4 yrs. exper.   14. _____

15. Pat, please type this memo [.] to the purchasing department.   15. _____

16. What? You lent that scoundrel Snively $10,000 [?!]   16. _____

17. I asked her why—of all the men on campus—she had chosen him [?]   17. _____

18. Why did I do it? Because I loved her [.] Alice was the finest person I've ever known.   18. _____

19. Footloose and Fancy Free [.] [title of an essay]   19. _____

20. Would you please send me your reply by return mail [.]   20. _____

21. Your cat ate my goldfish while I kept him for the weekend [!] Why didn't you tell me he was a
    murdering feline!   21. _____

22. Charlie was an inspiring [?] date. He had me yawning all night.   22. _____

23. "I can't [!] remember [!] her name," the socialite gasped as the poison took effect.   23. _____

24. You must bring the following: (1[.]) your bat, (2[.]) your glove, and (3[.]) your baseball shoes.   24. _____

25. I heard the news on station C[.]F[.]A[.]X.   25. _____

49. PUNCTUATION: THE SEMICOLON

(Study Section 39, The Semicolon.)

Using the following list, write the number of the **reason** for the semicolon in each sentence. (Use only one number in each blank.)

1. **between independent clauses *not* joined by any conjunction or conjunctive adverb**
2. **between independent clauses joined by a conjunctive adverb (*however, therefore,* etc.)**
3. **between clauses joined by *and, but, for, or, nor, so,* or *yet* but having internal commas**
4. **to group items in a series**

Example: Everyone predicts the Expos will win the World Series; John stills insists that the Jays will do it.   __1__

1. Parliament has now approved a bill to spend more to protect the ozone layer; however, it may be already too late.   1. _____

2. The farmers are using an improved fertilizer; thus their crop yields have increased.   2. _____

3. Still to come were Perry, a trained pig; Armand, an acrobat; and Marlene, a magician.   3. _____

4. "Negotiations," he said, "have collapsed; we will strike at noon."   4. _____

5. Read the questions carefully; answer each one as briefly as possible.   5. _____

6. A new liquid whole-egg product is on the market; this new product contains only 20 percent of the cholesterol of an egg.   6. _____

7. Pam, who lives in the suburbs, drives her car to work each day; yet Robin, her next-door neighbour, takes the bus.   7. _____

8. She had paid her dues; therefore, she was eligible to vote.   8. _____

9. The play was produced in Edmonton, Alberta; Vancouver, British Columbia; and Regina, Saskatchewan.   9. _____

10. Chris was a fatalist; she believed that all events were predetermined.   10. _____

If **a semicolon** is needed within the brackets, insert it; then in the blank at the right, write the number (**1** to **4** from the list above) of the **reason** for that semicolon.
If **no semicolon** is needed within the brackets, write **0** in the blank. (Use only one number in each blank.)

Example: I couldn't help you with your assignment[;] moreover, I wouldn't.   __2__

1. She is going to the concert on Friday[ ] do you want her to get tickets for us?   1. _____

2. Shall I telephone to find out the time[ ] when the box office opens?   2. _____

3. A recent study indicates that saccharin does not cause cancer in humans[ ] the only consumers who should worry are laboratory rats.   3. _____

4. Louise read the help wanted ads[ ] and went to the campus employment office for weeks until, to her great relief, she found a summer job.   4. _____

5. She is very gifted[ ] two of her poems appear in an anthology.   5. _____

6. The surprises in the team's starting lineup were Lansing, the second baseman[ ] Cordero, the short-stop[ ] and Fletcher, the catcher.

6. _____

7. The public education system needs to redefine its expectations[ ] because most schools don't expect all of their students to succeed.

7. _____

8. The subway was packed with commuters[ ] we had to stand.

8. _____

9. Her boardinghouse burned down[ ] consequently, she had to find new lodgings.

9. _____

10. The television series featuring childrearing strategies for the '90s is instructive[ ] but sometimes a bit unrealistic.

10. _____

50. PUNCTUATION: THE SEMICOLON AND THE COMMA

(Study Sections 30–32, The Comma, and Section 39, The Semicolon.)

Within the brackets, insert a comma, a semicolon, or nothing—whichever is **correct.** Then, in the blank at the right,

write **1** if you inserted **a comma** within the brackets;
write **2** if you inserted **a semicolon;**
write **0** if you inserted **nothing.**

(Use only one number in each blank.)

Example: The referee dropped the puck [ ] the game began.   <u> 2 </u>

1. Canadian workers are sometimes portrayed as being lazy [ ] still, Canadians generally have fewer vacation days than employees from other industrialized countries.   1. _____

2. Tony signed the petition to maintain the green space downtown [ ] but several of his friends argued that the city needed to use the space for a parking garage.   2. _____

3. Dr. Jones [ ] who teaches geology [ ] graduated from UBC.   3. _____

4. The Dr. Jones [ ] who teaches geology [ ] graduated from UBC.   4. _____

5. I met the woman [ ] who is to be president of the new junior college.   5. _____

6. She likes working in Arnprior, Ontario [ ] she hopes to remain there permanently.   6. _____

7. For the teenagers, the program was entertaining [ ] for the adults, it was boring.   7. _____

8. Read the article carefully [ ] then write an essay on the author's handling of the subject.   8. _____

9. The Japanese do have longer working hours [ ] in fact, they work 225 hours a year more than Canadian employees.   9. _____

10. The game being beyond our reach [ ] the coach told me to start warming up.   10. _____

11. We're going on a cruise around the bay on Sunday [ ] and we'd like you to come with us.   11. _____

12. If Amy decides to become a lawyer [ ] you can be sure she'll be a good one.   12. _____

13. I had worked in the library before [ ] therefore, I had no trouble getting a part-time job.   13. _____

14. Li-Young registered for an advanced biology course [ ] otherwise, she might not have been admitted to medical school.   14. _____

15. Some companies [ ] however [ ] are now using drug tests to screen job applicants.   15. _____

16. The new rug has been delivered [ ] but Terry is not pleased with its colour.   16. _____

17. He began his speech again [ ] fire engines having drowned out his opening remarks.   17. _____

18. On an international science test, the Canadian scores were quite low [ ] when compared with scores from other countries.   18. _____

19. Let me introduce the new officers: Elaine Schwartz, president [ ] Philip Donatelli, secretary [ ] and Kathy Romanow, treasurer.   19. _____

20. Children from the United States spend more time in the classroom than students from other industrialized nations [ ] yet Americans don't do as well on standardized tests when compared with their international peers.   20. _____

21. We had known the Floyd Archers [ ] ever since they moved here from New Brunswick. 21. _____

22. During that summer we visited friends in London [ ] New York [ ] and Toronto. 22. _____

23. The drama coach was a serene person [ ] not one to be worried by nervous amateurs. 23. _____

24. To turn them into professional performers was [ ] needless to say [ ] an impossible task. 24. _____

25. "Yes, I will attend the review session," Jack said [ ] "if you can guarantee that the time spent will be worthwhile." 25. _____

26. Call the security office [ ] if there seems to be any problem with the locks. 26. _____

27. Currently couples with severe disabilities may have difficulty raising a family [ ] because there are few programs to help disabled parents with their children. 27. _____

28. Britain was the first Common Market country to react [ ] others quickly followed suit. 28. _____

29. The tanker ran aground in perfectly fair weather and calm seas [ ] the captain was fired. 29. _____

30. Perhaps because Hitler had been an art student [ ] he commissioned many sculptures during the Nazi regime. 30. _____

31. The quadruple jump among ice skaters is still rare [ ] so far Elvis Stojko is the only skater to land one during international competition. 31. _____

32. The Stanley Cup hadn't yet begun [ ] however, he had equipped himself with a new television. 32. _____

33. I couldn't remember having seen her as radiantly happy [ ] as she now was. 33. _____

34. No, I cannot go to the game [ ] I have a term paper to finish. 34. _____

35. Ralf Socher [ ] in fact, is Canada's downhill skiing champion. 35. _____

36. Victor [ ] on the other hand [ ] played the best game of his career. 36. _____

37. Genevieve laughed hysterically [ ] Owen, on the other hand, was very serious. 37. _____

38. "There will be no rain today [ ]" she insisted. "The weather forecaster says so." 38. _____

39. Swimming is an excellent form of exercise [ ] swimming for twenty-six minutes consumes one hundred calories. 39. _____

40. Although he majored in math in college [ ] he has trouble dividing the lunch check. 40. _____

41. The short story [ ] that impressed me the most was [ ] written by a thirty-five-year-old police officer. 41. _____

42. Mary constantly counts calories and fat content in the food she eats [ ] yet she never loses a pound. 42. _____

43. Other cultures follow different calendars [ ] the Jewish New Year is celebrated in the fall and the Cambodian New Year in April. 43. _____

44. "My club [ ]" stated James, "completes numerous community service projects throughout the school year." 44. _____

45. Classes were well attended [ ] although many students were suffering with a flu virus. 45. _____

46. Muslim students on campus asked the administration for a larger international student centre [ ] and a quiet place for their daily prayers. 46. _____

47. Whenever I don't save a receipt [ ] I always end up needing to take back my purchase because it either doesn't fit or it's defective. 47. _____

48. Barry and I were planning a large farewell party for Eugene within the next month [ ] but certainly not for next week. 48. _____

49. To read only mysteries and novels [ ] was my plan for the holiday break. 49. _____

50. My German grandmother always kept an extremely clean, neat house; likewise [ ] my mother also spent a good portion of her day cleaning. 50. _____

51. PUNCTUATION: THE SEMICOLON AND THE COMMA

(Study Sections 30–32, The Comma, and Section 39, The Semicolon.)

Within the brackets, insert a comma, a semicolon, or nothing—whichever is **correct.** Then, in the blank at the right,

write **1** if you inserted **a comma** within the brackets;
write **2** if you inserted **a semicolon;**
write **0** if you inserted **nothing.**

(Use only one number in each blank.)

Example: The television blared [ ] the children sat motionless.　　　　　　　　__2__

1. Frank's father launched into his usual diatribe about the younger generation [ ] the room quickly emptied.　　1. _____

2. Recent members of Canada's women's ski team include Kate Pace [ ] Kerrin Lee–Gartner [ ] and Nanci Gee.　　2. _____

3. "Do you have any idea what will be on the final exam?" [ ] asked the student.　　3. _____

4. The lead runner crested the hill [ ] and glanced back at the others struggling far behind.　　4. _____

5. The score was tied [ ] the game would go into overtime.　　5. _____

6. Blenchford studied all night [ ] but failed the test.　　6. _____

7. Do you know, Professor Bullock [ ] where I could find a copy of the January issue of the *Journal of Reading*?　　7. _____

8. Unfortunately, the administration was located in an old [ ] dilapidated [ ] three-story building.　　8. _____

9. Time having run out [ ] I had to hand in my test paper before I had finished.　　9. _____

10. Vitamin D may be an important dietary supplement [ ] new studies link Vitamin D to the prevention of breast and colon cancer.　　10. _____

11. All farmers [ ] who have had their crops destroyed by this year's drought [ ] will be compensated.　　11. _____

12. Pursuing a hobby with other people with similar interests [ ] Jacob finally recovered from his depression.　　12. _____

13. She had been in the hospital [ ] therefore, she was behind in three weeks of classes.　　13. _____

14. During his first three years of college [ ] he attended three different schools.　　14. _____

15. Having learned that the meeting had been postponed [ ] John went back to the library.　　15. _____

16. Poised and completely at ease [ ] the student-body president greeted the new students.　　16. _____

17. "The answer is here somewhere," Holmes said [ ] "and I'm sure we can find it."　　17. _____

18. Most Canadians know about seasonal affective disorder (SAD) [ ] it's a recurrent depression linked to short, cold days.　　18. _____

19. Ms. Vane, the principal, waited [ ] until the students in the assembly hall were quiet.　　19. _____

20. The mayor adjusted his tie, smiled, and coughed [ ] then he said he was glad that the question had been asked.　　20. _____

21. Having my arm in a cast bothered me [ ] but the doctor insisted that a cast was necessary.　　21. _____

22. When traveling in another country, always pack some routine over-the-counter products [ ] you don't want to have to search for a bottle of aspirin in a foreign drugstore.

22. _____

23. Professor Curtis has left the campus [ ] however, she may be reached by telephone.

23. _____

24. This arrangement certainly is the best of all possible worlds [ ] don't you think?

24. _____

25. Exercising is really beneficial [ ] because it helps to reduce physical and psychological stress.

25. _____

26. After they graduated, they packed their belongings [ ] and moved to a small town in Quebec.

26. _____

27. Amy was aware as she raced down the hill [ ] that this event would be her last chance ever to win a medal in the downhill.

27. _____

28. He teaches first–year English [ ] Speech II [ ] and a literature course.

28. _____

29. Tuberculosis, Dr. Phillips[ ] will be the main focus for my research paper.

29. _____

30. Our representatives included Will Leeds, a member of the Rotary Club[ ] Tracy Allcott, a banker [ ] and Baldev Lalli, president of the Chamber of Commerce.

30. _____

31. Many companies are adding college-tuition assistance programs to their existing benefit packages [ ] and are providing on-site child care.

31. _____

32. She expects to graduate in June [ ] then she will spend her summer in Europe.

32. _____

33. He followed the trail to the summit [ ] later, he found the entrance to the mine.

33. _____

34. The computer virus destroyed the files on my hard drive [ ] and caused me to lose several days' worth of work.

34. _____

35. Without seeing where I made my mistakes on my essay [ ] I simply can't hope to do better next time.

35. _____

36. Peter lives in Prince Edward Island [ ] Howard in New Brunswick.

36. _____

37. The teacher asked [ ] that everyone be quiet.

37. _____

38. His adviser's signature being required [ ] Fred went to the administration building.

38. _____

39. Failing to make the right turn on the highway [ ] caused us to arrive two hours late.

39. _____

40. Fighting his way through a host of tacklers [ ] Curtis scored a touchdown.

40. _____

41. Dead-end jobs [ ] generally to be avoided by younger people [ ] may be perfect for retired senior citizens.

41. _____

42. When the party leader campaigned [ ] she promised three million new jobs.

42. _____

43. Upon graduating from college [ ] he went into the military.

43. _____

44. Vacation time is almost over [ ] there are only four days left.

44. _____

45. Since the economy seems to be improving [ ] economists predict that consumers will purchase more expensive items such as cars, stereo equipment, and jewelry.

45. _____

46. After attending his chemistry and psychology classes [ ] Leslie sat down to write a letter.

46. _____

47. Even after thirty years, Giovanni Giacommeti's metal sculptures are still well received by the public [ ] for each statue seems to capture life in the twentieth century.

47. _____

48. Frank was angry with Gail [ ] for having broken her promise to him to be prompt.

48. _____

49. He asked you to help him with his biology [ ] didn't he?

49. _____

50. They suspected that the leather jacket might be found [ ] if someone were to look through the gym lockers.

50. _____

52. PUNCTUATION: THE APOSTROPHE

(Study Sections 40–42, The Apostrophe.)

In the first column, write the number of the correct choice (**1** or **2**). In the second column, write the **number** (**3** to **6**, from the list below) of the **reason** for your choice. (If your choice has **no apostrophe,** write nothing in the second column.)

3. singular possessive   **5. contraction**
4. plural possessive   **6. plural of letter, number, symbol, word used as word**

Example: The day is (1) *our's* (2) *ours.*   2

1. I (1) *didn't* (2) *did'nt* have enough money with me to pay the taxi.   1. _____ _____

2. The (1) *Smith's* (2) *Smiths* have invited us to their daughter's wedding.   2. _____ _____

3. The (1) *James'* (2) *Jameses* are moving to Kelowna.   3. _____ _____

4. My (1) *brother-in-law's* (2) *brother's-in-law* wife is a pediatrician.   4. _____ _____

5. The (1) *Russo's* (2) *Russos* have a two-year-old son.   5. _____ _____

6. (1) *Its* (2) *It's* important to reduce the fat in your diet to 30 percent.   6. _____ _____

7. (1) *Who's* (2) *Whose* responsible for the increase in vandalism and violence in our
    public schools?   7. _____ _____

8. The two (1) *girl's* (2) *girls'* talent was quite evident to everyone.   8. _____ _____

9. We will be at the (1) *Lopez's* (2) *Lopezes'* home until midnight.   9. _____ _____

10. It will be a two-(1) *day's* (2) *days'* drive to the ocean.   10. _____ _____

11. He went on a three (1) *weeks'* (2) *week's* vacation trip to Hornby Island.   11. _____ _____

12. To get ahead, she planned to win her (1) *bosses* (2) *boss's* favour.   12. _____ _____

13. After the long absence, they fell into (1) *each others'* (2) *each other's* arms.   13. _____ _____

14. From its friendly greeting, it was evident that the dog was (1) *her's* (2) *hers.* 14. _____ _____

15. Verna uses too many (1) *ands* (2) *and's* in most of her speeches.   15. _____ _____

16. His (1) *O's* (2) *Os* have a solid black centre; his typewriter needs to be cleaned. 16. _____ _____

17. (1) *Wer'ent* (2) *Weren't* you surprised to see him so soon?   17. _____ _____

18. Which is safer, your school or (1) *ours* (2) *our's?*   18. _____ _____

19. Georgiana insisted, "I (1) *have'nt* (2) *haven't* seen Sandy for weeks."   19. _____ _____

20. He bought fifty (1) *cents* (2) *cents'* worth of popcorn.   20. _____ _____

21. The back alley was known to be a (1) *thieve's* (2) *thieves'* hangout.   21. _____ _____

22. There were far too many (1) *but's* (2) *buts* in his praise of my essay.   22. _____ _____

23. The (1) *children's* (2) *childrens'* computer was damaged in the last move.   23. _____ _____

24. "Your (1) *times* (2) *time's* up!" declared the little boy to the older girl on the swing. 24. _____ _____

25. The (1) *coal miner's* (2) *coal miners'* union went on strike for higher wages.   25. _____ _____

53. PUNCTUATION: THE APOSTROPHE

(**Study** Sections 40–42, The Apostrophe.)

For each bracketed apostrophe, write **1** if it is **correct**; write **0** if it is **incorrect**.

(**Use** the first column for the first apostrophe in each sentence; use the second column for the second apostrophe.)

	1	0
Example: *Who[']s* on first? Where's *todays [']* lineup?		
1. This is no one *else[']s* fault but *your[']s,* I'm sorry to say.	1. ____	____
2. Mrs. *Jackson[']s* invitation to the *William[']s* must have gone astray.	2. ____	____
3. He *would[']nt* know that after only two *day[']s* employment.	3. ____	____
4. *Wer[']en't* they fortunate that the damaged car wasn't *their[']s?*	4. ____	____
5. *It[']s* a pity that the one bad cabin would be *their[']s.*	5. ____	____
6. *We[']re* expecting the *Wagner[']s* to meet us in Whistler for a ski trip.	6. ____	____
7. "*Where[']s* your driver's license?" was the *officer[']s* first question.	7. ____	____
8. *Does[']nt* the student realize that he *won[']t* be able to submit all his papers so late?	8. ____	____
9. The two sisters had agreed that *they[']d* not wear each *others[']* clothes.	9. ____	____
10. *She[']s* not going to accept *anybody[']s* help, no matter how far behind she is on the project.	10. ____	____
11. The *childrens[']* prizes were distributed at the *Community High Schools[']* winter carnival.	11. ____	____
12. *He's* hoping to get two *hours[']* work each day in the school cafeteria.	12. ____	____
13. The idea of starting a scholarship fund was not *our[']s;* it was *Lois[']s.*	13. ____	____
14. There are three *i[']s* in the word *optimistic;* there are two *r[']s* in the word *embarrass.*	14. ____	____
15. The computer printout consisted of a series of *1[']s* and *0[']s.*	15. ____	____
16. Jack sent two dozen yellow *rose[']s* to the Women Student *Association[']s* meeting.	16. ____	____
17. I really *did[']nt* expect to see all of the *drivers[']* finish the race.	17. ____	____
18. Is it possible that you *have[']ent* heard about the fire at the *Jone[']s* house?	18. ____	____
19. The formerly popular *mens[']* store established in 1897 *was[']nt* able to compete with the large discount stores in the nearby mall.	19. ____	____
20. I'm sure that, if *he[']s* physically able, *he[']ll* play in next Saturday's football game.	20. ____	____
21. The responsibility for notifying club members is *her[']s,* not *our[']s.*	21. ____	____
22. *Can[']t* I persuade you that *you[']re* now financially able to own your own car?	22. ____	____
23. The *Olsons[']* understood that *we[']d* be late because of our schedule.	23. ____	____
24. The address on the envelope was not *our[']s;* it was the *Burgesses['].*	24. ____	____
25. My *mother-in-law[']s* books are aimed at a *children[']s* market.	25. ____	____

54. PUNCTUATION: THE APOSTROPHE

(Study Sections 40–42, The Apostrophe.)

In the paragraph below, every word ending in **s** has a number beneath it. In each corresponding blank after the paragraph,

write **1** if the word should end in **'s;**
write **2** if the word should end in **s':**
write **0** if the word needs **no apostrophe.**

Example: We took showers$_{40}$ after the game.

0

A junior hockey athletes$_1$ fondest dreams$_2$ concern being drafted by the professionals$_3$. If a teams$_4$ star averages$_5$ three or four points$_6$ a game or makes$_7$ an all-star team, that youngsters$_8$ phone rings$_9$ constantly, and his$_{10}$ mail carriers$_{11}$ bag overflows$_{12}$ with good wishes$_{13}$ from admirers$_{14}$. Yet very often this$_{15}$ young players$_{16}$ hopes$_{17}$ are falsely aroused by illusions$_{18}$ of riches$_{19}$ that turn out to be no better than an ordinary persons$_{20}$ salary. The medias$_{21}$ descriptions$_{22}$ of exciting arenas$_{23}$ overflowing with lively, eager members$_{24}$ of the opposite sex can stimulate a boys$_{25}$ imagination to the point where reality cannot match what the minds$_{26}$ eye envisions$_{27}$. The young players$_{28}$ disappointment becomes$_{29}$ all the keener when he learns$_{30}$ that the salary offers$_{31}$ from all the teams$_{32}$ are too low for the dreams$_{33}$ fulfillment.

1. ____ 10. ____ 19. ____ 28. ____
2. ____ 11. ____ 20. ____ 29. ____
3. ____ 12. ____ 21. ____ 30. ____
4. ____ 13. ____ 22. ____ 31. ____
5. ____ 14. ____ 23. ____ 32. ____
6. ____ 15. ____ 24. ____ 33. ____
7. ____ 16. ____ 25. ____
8. ____ 17. ____ 26. ____
9. ____ 18. ____ 27. ____

55. PUNCTUATION: ITALICS

(Study Section 43, Italics, [Underlining])

Write the number of the **reason** for each use of italics:

1. title of book, magazine, or newspaper
2. title of musical production, play, film, or TV show
3. name of ship, aircraft, or spacecraft
4. title of painting or sculpture

5. foreign word not yet Anglicized
6. word, letter, figure, or symbol referred to as such
7. emphasis

Example: I read nothing but *TV Guide.*   1. __1__

1. The *Titanic* was thought to be an unsinkable ship.   1. _____

2. *Peter Pan* seems to be shown on television every spring.   2. _____

3. For many years, the *Manchester Guardian* has been a leading newspaper in England.   3. _____

4. Much debate in the office was sparked by the recent rankings of universities in *Maclean's* magazine.   4. _____

5. Directions on the test indicated that all questions were to be answered with *1*'s or *2*'s.   5. _____

6. A mnemonic device for helping a student spell the word *principal* is the expression "The *principal* is your *pal.*"   6. _____

7. Susan learned to spell the word *villain* by thinking of a *villa in* Italy.   7. _____

8. She subscribes to *Vancouver, Ms.,* and *Harrowsmith* magazines.   8. _____

9. The Aboriginal Art Exhibit will feature *Daily Lives,* carvings by the people of Rankin Inlet.   9. _____

10. An article had been written recently about the frigate *Esquimault.*   10. _____

11. Gloria Steinem, one of the founders of modern American feminism, has published several books, including *Revolution from Within.*   11. _____

12. How many *s*'s and *i*'s are there in Mississippi?   12. _____

13. Many Canadian sports fans consider *The Hockey News* one of their favourite newspapers.   13. _____

14. The American pronunciation of *schedule* is *skedule;* the Canadian pronunciation is either that or *shedule.*   14. _____

15. Peter Cook is a regular contributor to *The Report on Business* and has written several columns a week for many years.   15. _____

16. Even though Canadian women now lead very busy lives, they are learning to say *no* to many professional demands so that they can enjoy their families and friends more.   16. _____

17. Aboard the *Enterprise,* the captain made plans to return to the planet Zircon to rescue Mr. Spock.   17. _____

18. He has a leading role in the opera *Pagliacci,* hasn't he?   18. _____

19. She went to Italy aboard the luxury liner *Michelangelo.*   19. _____

20. She orbited the earth in the *Columbia* shuttle.   20. _____

21. Her printed *R*'s and *B*'s closely resemble each other.   21. _____

22. Although he never held office, Lopez was the *de facto* ruler of his country.   22. _____

23. Some people spell and pronounce the words *athlete* and *athletics* as if there were an *e* after *th* in each word.   23. _____

24. *Prelude to a Kiss* is a movie about a contemporary fairy tale set in the uncertain world of the 1990s.

24. _____

25. The original meaning of the word *mad* was "disordered in mind" or "insane."

25. _____

In each sentence there is **one** word or set of words that should be italicized. Underline these words, and write in the blank the number (**1** to **7**, from the list on page 000) of the **reason** for the italics.

Example: We were all on the cover of *Newsweek*.   <u>1</u>

1. "First We Take Manhattan" is a cut on Leonard Cohen's CD I'm Your Man.   1. _____

2. Deciding to come home by ship, we made reservations on the Queen Elizabeth II.   2. _____

3. Gerry went downtown to buy copies of MacWorld, Chatelaine, and Family Circle.   3. _____

4. "It's time for a change," affirmed the candidate during the debate.   4. _____

5. Showboat, a revival of a 1940s musical, has done well both in Toronto and on Broadway.   5. _____

6. The Toronto Star must have weighed five pounds last Saturday.   6. _____

7. The Kids in the Hall on CBC never fails to be outrageously funny.   7. _____

8. Richler's Solomon Gusrky Was Here has become one of my favourite books.   8. _____

9. Among the magazines lying on the table was a copy of Geo.   9. _____

10. Jane Urquhart's acclaimed novel, Away, has been a Canadian best seller for over a year.   10. _____

11. When I try to pronounce the word statistics, I always stumble over it.   11. _____

12. She seems unaware of the difference between the words accept and except.   12. _____

13. "There is no such word as alright," said Dr. Williams, as she wrote the sentence on the chalkboard.   13. _____

14. Picasso's Guernica depicts the horrors of war.   14. _____

15. The Thinker is a statute that many people admire.   15. _____

16. Lawrence of Arabia is considered an outstanding motion picture of the 1960s.   16. _____

17. You'll enjoy reading "The Man of the House" in the book Fifty Great Short Stories.   17. _____

18. The American spelling of the word humour is h-u-m-o-r.   18. _____

19. "What is College For?" is an essay by Max McConn in Modern English Readings.   19. _____

20. Michelangelo's Last Judgement shows "the omnipotence of his artistic ability."   20. _____

21. The source of the above quotation is the Canadian Encyclopedia.   21. _____

22. The fourth opera in this winter's series is Verdi's Don Carlo.   22. _____

23. Her argument was ad hominem.   23. _____

24. Perry won the spelling bee's award for creative expression with his rendition of antidisestablishmentarianism.   24. _____

25. The instructor said that Sam's 7's and his 4's look very much alike.   25. _____

56. PUNCTUATION: QUOTATION MARKS

(Study Sections 44–48, Quotation Marks)

Insert **quotation marks** (double or single, as needed) at the proper places in each sentence. Then, in the blank at the right, write the number (1 to **12** from the list below) of the **reason** for the quotation marks:

1. **direct quotation**
2. **title of chapter**
3. **title of magazine article**
4. **title of short story**
5. **title of essay**
6. **title of poem**
7. **title of song**
8. **title of one-act play**
9. **title of lecture**
10. **title of newspaper article or editorial**
11. **definition**
12. **nickname**

Example: My childhood nickname "Stringbean" no longer fits me.   <u>12</u>

1. The article about silk, The Queen of Textiles, appeared in *National Geographic* magazine in January 1984.   1. _____

2. The Ugly Truth which appeared in *Saturday Night* magazine, tells the story of a feisty investigative reporter.   2. _____

3. W. C. Fields' dying words were I'd rather be in Philadelphia.   3. _____

4. The poem The Swing was written by Robert Louis Stevenson.   4. _____

5. Be prepared, warned the weather forecaster, for a particularly harsh winter this year.   5. _____

6. In the Chute is a chapter in the novel *An Occasional Cow.*   6. _____

7. In the magazine *Island Parent,* Susan Bryce, in an article titled The First Two Years, discusses how to make a home childproof.   7. _____

8. The word *cavalier* was originally defined as a man on a horse.   8. _____

9. Wayne The Moose Larson took both players into the boards.   9. _____

10. Silent Night is a song heard frequently during the Christmas season.   10. _____

11. One of my favourite short stories is Clark Blaise's I'm Dreaming of Rocket Richard.   11. _____

12. Did the professor give the lecture Abnormal Behavior last semester?   12. _____

13. The World Is Too Much with Us is a poem by William Wordsworth.   13. _____

14. The Foothills is an article that appeared in *Equinox* magazine.   14. _____

15. An article that appeared in the *Calgary Sun* is How Much Is There Left To Cut?   15. _____

16. Bacon's essay Of Fortune comments sadly on the brevity of human friendship.   16. _____

17. The Love Song of J. Alfred Prufrock is a poem by T. S. Eliot.   17. _____

18. Moonlodge is a one-actor play by Margo Kane.   18. _____

19. The concluding song of the evening was Auld Lang Syne.   19. _____

20. We read a poem by P.K. Page entitled The Stenographers.   20. _____

21. The Inner Harbour Renewal is the title of an editorial in *The Times Colonist.*   21. _____

22. Tom had private tutoring from Ezell The Disk Man Adams.   22. _____

23. We read House Breaking, an essay by Charlotte Gray.

23. _____

24. She enjoyed Arthur Foff's short story Beautiful Golden-Haired Mamie.

24. _____

25. *Discography* means a comprehensive list of recordings made by a particular performer or of a particular composer's work.

25. _____

57. PUNCTUATION: QUOTATION MARKS

(Study Sections 44–48, Quotation Marks.)

Write **1** if the punctuation in brackets is **correct.**
Write **0** if it is **incorrect.**
(Use only one number in each blank.)

Example: "Want to play ball, Scarecrow [?]" the Wicked Witch asked, a ball of fire in her hand.   __1__

1. The late arrivals asked [,"] When did the party end?"   1. _____

2. When the job was finished, the worker asked, "How do you like it [?"]   2. _____

3. In the first semester, we read Joyce's "The Dead ["].   3. _____

4. "Where are you now employed? [",] the interviewer asked.   4. _____

5. "When you finish your rough draft," said Professor Grill [,"] bring it by my office."   5. _____

6. Who was it who mused, "Where are the snows of yesteryear ["?]   6. _____

7. Dr. Nelson, our political science teacher, asked, "How many of you have read *The October Crisis*[?"]   7. _____

8. "Canadians need education and jobs [,"] exclaimed the college student.   8. _____

9. "Write when you can [,"] Mother said as I left for the airport.   9. _____

10. To *sympathize* means ["] to share in suffering or grief ["].   10. _____

11. "Ask not what your country can do for you [;"] ask what you can do for your country."   11. _____

12. "Our language creates problems when we talk about gender. ["] ["] We don't have enough terms to explain the complexities of the issues."   12. _____

13. "Do you remember Father's saying, 'Never give up [?'] she asked.   13. _____

14. She began reciting the opening lines of one of Elizabeth Barrett Browning's sonnets: "How do I love thee? Let me count the ways ["].   14. _____

15. Irving Layton's poem ["] Song for Naomi ["] is one of his best.   15. _____

16. ["]*Billy Bishop Goes To War* ["] is one of the most successful musical plays in Canadian theatre.   16. _____

17. Annette said, "Don't you get tired of hearing karaoke performers butcher `Unchained Melody [?'"]   17. _____

18. "Shall I read aloud Eva Tihanyi's poem, 'Blind Man ['?"] she asked.   18. _____

19. Have you read Bill Bissett's poem "Grade School in Halifax [?"]   19. _____

20. When Susan saw the show about Canada's poor, she exclaimed "I have to find a way to help [!"]   20. _____

21. The noun *neurotic* is defined as "an emotionally unstable individual ["].   21. _____

22. "I'm going to the newsstand," he said [;"] for a copy of the *Equinox.*"   22. _____

23. "Do you believe in fairies [?"] Peter Pan asks the children.   23. _____

24. How maddening of her to reply calmly, "You're so right ["!]   24. _____

25. "Come as soon as you can," said Mother to the plumber [. "]The basement is already flooded."   25. _____

26. I heard Andy say, James asked, 'Who are the new neighbours down the street ['"]   26. _____

27. "The Management of Grief [,"] a short story by Bharti Mukherjee, was discussed in Janet's English class.   27. _____

28. Did you read Krutch's article, "Is the Common Man Too Common? ["?]   28. _____

29. "Was the treaty signed in 1815 [?"] the professor asked, "or in 1814?"   29. _____

30. The contractor said, "I guarantee that the renovation will move forward rapidly [;"] however, I don't believe him.   30. _____

31. Clark Blaise writes: "The first sentence of a story is an act of faith—or astonishing bravado ["."]   31. _____

32. "Have you seen the rough draft of the article?" asked Jackie [?]   32. _____

33. I reread Audrey Thomas' "Basmati Rice: An Essay About Words ["."]   33. _____

58. PUNCTUATION: ITALICS AND QUOTATION MARKS

(Study Section 43, Italics, and 44–48, Quotation Marks.)

Write the number of the **correct** choice.

Example: A revival of (1) *Show Boat* (2)"Show Boat" is playing at the Ford Theatre.   1
_____

1. (1) "Cats,"(2) *Cats,* which is one of Canada's most successful productions, is based on the work of T. S. Eliot.   1. _____

2. An editorial titled (1) *Public Transit Needs Public Money* (2) "Public Transit Needs Public Money" appeared in the *Hamilton Spectator.*   2. _____

3. (1) "London Bridge" (2) *London Bridge* is a popular nursery rhyme.   3. _____

4. Paul Kennedy's book (1) *The Rise and Fall of the Great Powers* (2) "The Rise and Fall of the Great Powers" discusses how nations become politically and militarily dominant.   4. _____

5. The title of the *Maclean's* article is (1) *Unexpected Satisfactions* (2) "Unexpected Satisfactions."   5. _____

6. The closing song of the concert was (1) "R-E-S-P-E-C-T" (2) *R-E-S-P-E-C-T.*   6. _____

7. (1) *Hairball* (2) "Hairball" is a short story by Margaret Atwood.   7. _____

8. The subject of Jay MacPherson's poem (1) *Eve in Reflection* (2) "Eve in Reflection" appealed to her.   8. _____

9. Helen received (1) *A's* (2) "A's" in three of her classes this fall.   9. _____

10. She used too many (1) *and's* (2) "and's" in her introductory speech.   10. _____

11. (1) *Science and Religion* (2) "Science and Religion" is an essay by Albert Einstein.   11. _____

12. He has purchased tickets for the opera (1) "Faust" (2) *Faust.*   12. _____

13. Sharon didn't use a spell-check program and, therefore, unfortunately misspelled (1) *psychology* (2) "psychology" throughout her paper.   13. _____

14. Dr. Baylor spent an entire class on E. J. Pratt's poem (1) "Sea-Gulls" (2) *Sea-Gulls.*   14. _____

15. His favourite newspaper has always been the (1) *Times* (2) "Times."   15. _____

16. (1) "Les Belles-Soeurs" (2) *Les Belles-Soeurs* is a play by Michel Tremblay.   16. _____

17. The word *altogether* means (1) "wholly" or "thoroughly" (2) *wholly* or *thoroughly.*   17. _____

18. (1) *What Women Want* (2) "What Women Want" is an essay by Margaret Mead.   18. _____

19. Steven Leacock's short story, (1) *My Financial Career* (2) "My Financial Career" amused her.   19. _____

20. The Players' Guild will produce Marlowe's (1) *Dr. Faustus* (2) "Dr. Faustus" next month.   20. _____

21. Edward Tomlinson's's article (1) *Will the Expos Move?* (2) "Will the Expos Move?" appeared in the January 1995 edition of the *Sporting News.*   21. _____

22. (1) *Biology: Science of Life* (2) "Biology: Science of Life" is our very expensive textbook for biochemistry class.   22. _____

23. One of the first readings for our Canadian political science class was David Bercuson's book (1) *Deconfederation* (2) "Deconfederation."   23. _____

24. Our film class saw Truffaut's (1) *Shoot the Piano Player* (2) "Shoot the Piano Player" last week.   24. _____

25. She read (1) *Dover Beach,* (2) "Dover Beach," a poem by Matthew Arnold.   25. _____

26. (1) *Pygmalion* (2) "Pygmalion" is a play by George Bernard Shaw.   26. _____

27. You fail to distinguish between the words (1)*range* and *vary* (2) "range" and "vary."   27. _____

28. I read a poem by Yeats titled (1) "The Cat and the Moon" (2) *The Cat and the Moon.*   28. _____

29. Madeline decided to treat herself by ordering a subscription to (1) *Reader's Digest* (2) Reader's
Digest."   29. _____

30. (1) *Bound East for Cardiff* (2) "Bound East for Cardiff" is a one-act play by O'Neill.   30. _____

31. I used (1) "Do Lie Detectors Lie?" (2) *Do Lie Detectors Lie?* from *Science* to write my report
on famous murder trials.   31. _____

32. Through Stuart McLean's book (1) "Welcome Home," (2) *Welcome Home,* readers have a chance
to see how Canadians from all provinces and territories think about their lives.   32. _____

33. Virginia Woolf's essay (1) "Professions for Women" (2) *Professions for Women* was first delivered
as a speech to a group of upper-class women, who were just beginning careers.   33. _____

59. PUNCTUATION: THE COLON, THE DASH, PARENTHESES, AND BRACKETS

(Study Sections 49–50, The Colon; Section 51, The Dash; Sections 52–53, Parentheses; and Section 54, Brackets.)

The Colon

Write **1** if the colon in brackets is used **correctly.**
Write **0** if it is used **incorrectly.**

Example: We invited [:] Larry, Moe, and Curly.   0

1. Casey's first question was [:] Can anybody here play this game?   1. _____

2. The coach signaled the strategy [:] we would try a double steal on the next pitch.   2. _____

3. Dear Sir [:] My five years' experience as a physician's assistant qualifies me for the position
   advertised.   3. _____

4. Dear "Stretch" [:] The whole group—all eight of us—plan to spend the weekend with you.   4. _____

5. Laurie's shopping list included these items [:] truffles, caviar, champagne, and a dozen hot dogs.   5. _____

6. The carpenter brought his [:] saw, hammer, square, measuring tape, and nails.   6. _____

7. College students generally complain about [:] their professors, the cafeteria food, and their
   roommates.   7. _____

8. She began her letter to Tom with these words [:] "You are a stupid fool!"   8. _____

9. I knew that her plane left on Tuesday at approximately 3 [:] 30 p.m.   9. _____

10. The athletic director demanded that [:] the coaches, the players, and the training staff meet with
    him immediately.   10. _____

11. Tonight's winning 6/49 numbers are [:] 3, 5, 21, 26 30, and 43.   11. _____

12. She was warned that the project would require one thing [:] perseverance.   12. _____

13. The report has been delayed [:] the chair has been hospitalized because of emergency surgery.   13. _____

14. The president of the university declared [:] "The Clearihue Building, the oldest structure on campus,
    will be rebuilt despite the extensive fire damage."   14. _____

15. I packed my suitcase with [:] bubble bath, a couple of novels, and my business clothes.   15. _____

The Dash, Parentheses, and Brackets

Set off the boldface words by inserting the **correct** punctuation. Then write the number of the punctuation
you inserted:

1. dash(es)   2. parentheses   3. brackets

Example: Jack Frazer **Ref. Saanich** voted for the proposal.   2

1. It's raining too hard to go to school today **just look out the window.**   1. _____

2. Holmes had deduced **who knew how?** that the man had been born on a moving train during the
   rainy season. [Punctuate to indicate a sharp interruption.]   2. _____

3. He will be considered for **this is between you and me, of course** one of the three vice-presidencies in the firm. [Punctuate to indicate merely incidental comment.]

3. _____

4. I simply told her **and I'm glad I did!** that I would never set foot in her house again. [Punctuate to indicate merely incidental comment.]

4. _____

5. Within the last year, I have received three **or was it four?** letters from her. [Punctuate to indicate merely incidental comment.]

5. _____

6. At Glacier National Park we watched the feeding of the bears **from a safe distance, you can be sure.** [Punctuate to achieve a dramatic effect.]

6. _____

7. Her essay was entitled "The Canadian Medicare System and It's **sic** Problems."

7. _____

8. The rules for using parentheses **see page 7** are not difficult to master.

8. _____

9. Only one thing stood in the way of buying a personal computer **credit**.

9. _____

10. The statement read: "Enclosed you will find one hundred dollars **$100** to cover damages."

10. _____

11. David liked one kind of dessert **apple pie.**

11. _____

12. **Eat, drink, and be merry** gosh, I can hardly wait for study week.

12. _____

13. The essay begins: "For more than a hundred years **from 1337 until 1453** the British and French fought a pointless war." [Punctuate to show that the boldface expression is inserted editorially.]

13. _____

14. The Stones concert begins at **by the way, when does the Stones concert begin?**

14. _____

15. Getting to work at eight o'clock every morning **I don't have to remind you how much I dislike getting up early** seemed almost more than I care to undertake. [Punctuate to indicate merely incidental comment.]

15. _____

16. She said, "Two of my friends **one has really serious emotional problems** need psychiatric help." [Punctuate to achieve a dramatic effect.]

16. _____

17. Campbell's work on Juvenal **see reference** is an excellent place to start.

17. _____

18. Dunsmuir was born in 1900 **?** and came west as a young boy.

18. _____

60. PUNCTUATION: THE HYPHEN

(Study Section 55, The Hyphen.)

Write **1** if the use or omission of a hyphen is **correct.**
Write **0** if it is **incorrect.**

Example: *Seventy six* trombones led the big parade.	0
1. Mr. Pollard's major research interest was *seventeenth-century* French history.	1. _____
2. Dana made a *semi-serious* effort to pick up the check.	2. _____
3. "I *c-c-can't* breathe because of my asthma," panted the patient.	3. _____
4. The *six-year-old* boy climbed onto the speaker's platform and sat down.	4. _____
5. She rented a *two room* apartment close to campus.	5. _____
6. The speaker was *well known* to everyone connected with administration.	6. _____
7. A *well-known* scientist will conduct a seminar during summer session.	7. _____
8. The team averaged over *fifty-thousand* spectators a game.	8. _____
9. The contractor expects to build many *five-* and *six-room* houses this year.	9. _____
10. The club president sent a *skillfully worded* statement to the city editor.	10. _____
11. I sent in my subscription to a new *bi-monthly* magazine.	11. _____
12. Sam's *brother-in-law* promised to help clean out the hunting lodge before deer season.	12. _____
13. At last her dream of an *up to date* kitchen was coming true.	13. _____
14. He made every effort to *recover* the missing gems.	14. _____
15. Because she lost her floppy disk, she had to *re-write* her report.	15. _____
16. At *eighty-one,* Hartley still rode his motorcycle in the mountains.	16. _____
17. Charles will run in the *hundred yard* dash next Saturday.	17. _____
18. "The children are not to have any more *c-a-n-d-y,*" said Mom.	18. _____
19. After he graduated from college, he became manager of the *student-owned* bookstore.	19. _____
20. The idea of a *thirty hour* week appealed to the workers.	20. _____
21. Baird played *semi-professional* baseball before going into the major leagues.	21. _____
22. Customers began avoiding the *hot-tempered* clerk in the shoe department.	22. _____
23. His friends tried to restore Al's *self-confidence.*	23. _____
24. The *brand-new* personal computer was faster than any of the other systems in the lab.	24. _____
25. The word processing software was *brand new.*	25. _____

61. PUNCTUATION: REVIEW

(Study Sections 30–55, Punctuation.)

Write **1** for each statement that is **true.**
Write **0** for each that is **false.**

Example: A **period** is used at the end of a declarative statement.   <u> 1 </u>

1. **Single quotation marks** are used to enclose a quotation within a quotation.   1. _____

2. An **apostrophe** is used to indicate the possessive case of personal pronouns.   2. _____

3. The **question mark** is always placed *inside* closing quotation marks.   3. _____

4. A **dash** may be indicated by the use of two hyphens on the typewriter.   4. _____

5. A **dash** is used before the author's name following a direct quotation.   5. _____

6. **Parentheses** are used to enclose editorial remarks in a direct quotation.   6. _____

7. **No commas** are used to set off a restrictive adjective clause.   7. _____

8. A **semicolon** is used to set off an absolute phrase from the rest of the sentence.   8. _____

9. The use of **brackets** around the word *sic* indicates an error occurring in quoted material.   9. _____

10. Mild interjections should be followed by an **exclamation point;** strong ones, by a **comma.**   10. _____

11. An indirect question is followed by a **period.**   11. _____

12. A **semicolon** is used after the expression *Dear Sir.*   12. _____

13. The title of a magazine article should be underlined to designate the use of **italics.**   13. _____

14. **Ms.** takes a period but **Miss** does not.   14. _____

15. The title of a newspaper is enclosed in **double quotation marks.**   15. _____

16. *Mr. Jone's, Mr. Jones',* and *Mr. Jones's* are all acceptable **possessive** forms of *Mr. Jones.*   16. _____

17. The title at the head of a composition should be enclosed in **double quotation marks.**   17. _____

18. **No apostrophe** is needed in the following greeting: "Merry Christmas from the Palmers."   18. _____

19. The **possessive** of *somebody else* is *somebody's else.*   19. _____

20. The **possessive** of *mother-in-law* is *mother's-in-law*   20. _____

21. A **semicolon** is used between two independent clauses joined by *and* if one or both clauses contain internal commas.   21. _____

22. A quotation consisting of several sentences takes ***double quotation marks*** at the beginning of the first sentence and at the end of the last sentence.   22. _____

23. A quotation consisting of several paragraphs takes **double quotation marks** at the beginning and end of each paragraph.   23. _____

24. The **plurals** of words, letters, or numbers (referred to as such) are formed by the addition of 's to the singular form.   24. _____

25. The word *the* is **italicized** in the name of a newspaper or a magazine.   25. _____

26. A polite request in the form of a question is followed by a **period.**   26. _____

27. **Single quotation marks** may be substituted for double quotation marks around any quoted passage.

27. _____

28. The **comma** is always placed *outside* quotation marks.

28. _____

29. The **colon** and **semicolon** are always placed *inside* quotation marks.

29. _____

30. A **comma** is always used to separate the two parts of a compound predicate.

30. _____

31. The expression *such as* is always followed by a **comma.**

31. _____

32. The nonsentence is a legitimate unit of expression and may be followed by a **period.**

32. _____

33. When a declarative sentence is followed by a confirmatory question, a **comma** is used between them.

33. _____

34. **Parentheses** are used around words that are to be deleted from a manuscript.

34. _____

35. A **comma** is used between two independent clauses not joined by a coordinating conjunction.

35. _____

36. A *semicolon* is used after the salutation of a business letter.

36. _____

37. The subject of a sentence should be separated from the predicate by use of a *comma.*

37. _____

38. An overuse of *underlining* (italics) for emphasis should be avoided.

38. _____

39. The **contraction** of the words *have not* is written thus: *hav'ent.*

39. _____

40. Nonrestrictive clauses are always set off with **commas.**

40. _____

41. **Double quotation marks** are used around the name of a ship.

41. _____

42. A **comma** is used before the word *then* when it introduces a second clause.

42. _____

43. The prefix *semi-* always requires a **hyphen.**

43. _____

44. *No comma* is required in the following sentence: "Where do you wish to go?" he asked.

44. _____

45. A **dash** is a legitimate substitute for all other marks of punctuation.

45. _____

46. A **hyphen** is used between two parts of a written-out number from 21 to 99.

46. _____

47. Names of persons directly addressed are set off by a **comma** (or **commas**).

47. _____

48. Every introductory prepositional phrase is set off by a **comma.**

48. _____

49. An introductory adverbial clause is set off with a **comma.**

49. _____

50. A *colon* may be used instead of a *semicolon* between two independent clauses when the second clause is an explanation of the first.

50. _____

62. PUNCTUATION: REVIEW

(Study Sections 30–55, Punctuation.)

Write **1** if the punctuation in brackets is **correct.**
Write **0** if it is **incorrect.**
(Use only one number in each blank.)

Example: The church bells[,] have been ringing all morning.   0

1. He found math difficult[;] but, because he worked so hard, he earned a *B*.   1. _____

2. The Messicks were late[,] their car battery having gone dead.   2. _____

3. I wondered what Shirley was doing[?]   3. _____

4. Dear Dr. Stanley[;] Thank you for your letter of May 10.   4. _____

5. Nick enjoyed inviting his friends[,] and preparing elaborate meals for them; however, most of his attempts were disasters.   5. _____

6. When the salesman described the new computer, everyone asked, "How much will it cost us["?]   6. _____

7. I remembered the job counselor's remark: "If you send out three hundred inquiry letters in your hometown without even one response, relocate[!"]   7. _____

8. "Despite the recession," explained the placement counselor[,] "tourism, construction, and business services still promise an increase in employment opportunities."   8. _____

9. A novella by Conrad, a short story by Lawrence, and some poems of Yeats[,] were all assigned for the last week of the semester.   9. _____

10. She arrived in Sudbury, Ontario[,] last Saturday.   10. _____

11. The chemistry department's grant proposal was better written than our[']s.   11. _____

12. The relief workers specifically requested food, blankets, and children[s'] clothing.   12. _____

13. He opened his briefcase[,] he took out his notes and began to talk.   13. _____

14. Whenever he speaks, he's inclined to use too many *and-uh*[']s between sentences.   14. _____

15. The Brentwood Bay area has been slowly deteriorating[;] because of a significant increase in real estate development that has increased the amount of sewage in the region.   15. _____

16. The last employee to leave the office is responsible for the following[,] turning off all machines, extinguishing all lights, and locking all executives' office doors.   16. _____

17. Everywhere there were crowds shouting anti[-]American slogans.   17. _____

18. This game is the one all Canada[']s been waiting for—the seventh game of the Stanley Cup final.   18. _____

19. During the whole wretched ordeal of his trial[;] Charles remained outwardly calm.   19. _____

20. More than twenty minutes were cut from the original version of the film[,] the producers told neither the director nor the writer.   20. _____

21. June 1, 1990[,] is the date we left Montreal.   21. _____

22. The fugitive was arrested near Melville, Saskatchewan[,] in a deserted farmhouse.   22. _____

23. The temperature sinking fast as dusk approached[;] we decided to seek shelter for the night.   23. _____

24. MacArthur's forces landed at Inchon[;] thus cutting off the North Koreans.   24. _____

25. My only cousin [,] who is in the Armed Forces[,] is stationed in the Arctic.   25. _____

26. Any Armed Forces officer[,] who is stationed in the Arctic [,] receives extra pay.   26. _____

27. Hey! Did you find a biology book in this classroom [?!]   27. _____

28. In Malibu, California, whales, dolphins, and porpoises have been granted citizenship [,] the Malibu City Council hopes to protect these cetaceans from exploitation by researchers and the armed services.   28. _____

29. Murphy's boss commended him on his frankness and spunk [;] then he fired Murphy.   29. _____

30. He wanted [,] to tell the truth [,] but lacked the courage.   30. _____

31. Jay jumped and squealed with delight [,] because he found a new pair of roller blades under his bed as a birthday present from his family.   31. _____

32. The movies [,] that I prefer to see [,] always have happy endings.   32. _____

33. At the Powwow [;] Anna and her friends entered the Fancy Shawl Dance competition, for they wanted to dance in their new dresses and moccasins.   33. _____

63. MECHANICS: CAPITALS

(Study Sections 61–63, Capitalization.)

Write **1** if the boldface words are correct in use or omission of capital letters.
Write **0** if they are **incorrect.**

Example: Cajuns speak a dialect of *french.* ____0____

1. They met at the North Side *Jewish* Center. 1. _____
2. My brother teaches *high school.* 2. _____
3. The *turkish* bath is closed. 3. _____
4. Hyeon Woo's uncle is a Buddhist *Monk.* 4. _____
5. When will *Parliament* sit? 5. _____
6. She is a *student* at Western. 6. _____
7. My *daughter* graduated from Memorial University. 7. _____
8. He always disliked *Algebra.* 8. _____
9. Mars is the *god* of war. 9. _____
10. I made an appointment with *Professor* Allen. 10. _____
11. She met three *Professors* today. 11. _____
12. "Did you save your paper on disk?" *she* asked. 12. _____
13. Each *Fall* I try to learn something new. 13. _____
14. The deaths were reported in the **Gazette.** 14. _____
15. I was born in the *Arctic.* 15. _____
16. Her *Aunt Miriam* has returned. 16. _____
17. He's late for his *economics* class. 17. _____
18. Jane was *President* of her club. 18. _____
19. Woods was promoted to *Major.* 19. _____
20. My *Grandfather* wrote to me. 20. _____
21. I enrolled in *english* and calculus. 21. _____
22. He began his letter with "My *Dear* Mrs. Johnson." 22. _____
23. He ended it with "Yours *Truly.*" 23. _____

24. We once lived in the *Northwest.* 24. _____
25. I passed German but failed *Calculus.* 25. _____
26. He entered *College* last fall. 26. _____
27. My *mother* is a lawyer. 27. _____
28. I asked *Mother* for some legal advice. 28. _____
29. He goes to *Cedar Hill High School.* 29. _____
30. Has the *commons* elected a speaker yet? 30. _____
31. The Cohens are now *Senior* citizens. 31. _____
32. The chess champion is from the *Junior Class.* 32. _____
33. Cecilia is a *teacher* in high school. 33. _____
34. I spent the fall break with my *Cousin.* 34. _____
35. Her favourite subject is *french.* 35. _____
36. The tourists visited the *Grand Canyon.* 36. _____
37. I traveled *South* for vacation. 37. _____
38. He enrolled in *Physics 2.* 38. _____
39. This is the *Anglican Church.* 39. _____
40. I saw Sid (*What* is his last name?) downstairs. 40. _____
41. This is *NOT* my idea of fun. 41. _____
42. The carton of *disks* was damaged. 42. _____
43. She earned a *Ph.D.* degree. 43. _____
44. The *World Series* has ended. 44. _____
45. She declared that charity is a *Christian* value. 45. _____
46. His father fought bravely in the Korean *war.* 46. _____

47. The chairperson of the **Department of Computer Sciences** is Dr. MacIntosh.

47. _____

48. He said simply, "*my* name is Bond."

48. _____

49. "**Sexual Harassment: The Price of Silence**" is a chapter from my composition reader.

49. _____

50. She spent her **Thanksgiving** vacation in Victoria with her cousins.

50. _____

64. MECHANICS: CAPITALS

(Study Sections 61–63, Capitalization.)

In the first column, write the number of the **first correct** choice (**1** or **2**).
In the second column, write the number of the second correct choice (**3** or **4**).

Example: Wandering (1) *West* (2) *west,* Max met (3) *Milly* (4) *milly.*   <u> 2 </u> <u> 3 </u>

1. Eaton's Department (1) *Store* (2) *store* is having a great sale on Italian (3) *Shoes*
   (4) *shoes.*   1. ———— ————

2. Her (1) *Father* (2) *father* went (3) *West* (4) *west* on business.   2. ———— ————

3. The new (1) *College* (2) *college* is seeking a (3) *President* (4) *president.*   3. ———— ————

4. We are taught to begin letters with "My (1) *Dear* (2) *dear* (3) *Sir* (4) *sir.*"   4. ———— ————

5. Business letters often end with "Very (1) *Truly* (2) *truly* (3) *Yours* (4) *yours.*"   5. ———— ————

6. After (1) *Church* (2) *church* we walked across the Ambassador (3) *Bridge* (4) *bridge.*   6. ———— ————

7. The (1) *Headwaiter* (2) *headwaiter* bowed deferentially to the (3) *Royal* (4) *royal* guests. 7. ———— ————

8. The young (1) *Lieutenant* (2) *lieutenant* prayed to the (3) *Lord* (4) *lord* for courage in
   the coming battle.   8. ———— ————

9. My (1) *Sister* (2) *sister* now lives in the (3) *East* (4) *east.*   9. ———— ————

10. The (1) *Prime Minister* (2) *prime minister* won't be in (3) *Parliament* (4) *parliament*
    tomorrow.   10. ———— ————

11. Edna Barney, (1) *M.D.* (2) *m.d.,* once taught (3) *Biology 4* (4) *biology 4.*   11. ———— ————

12. Dr. Sherwood, (1) *Professor* (2) *professor* of (3) *English* (4) *english,* is now on leave. 12. ———— ————

13. Students graduating from Mountain School frequently do well in (1) *French* (2) *french*
    and (3) *Math* (4) *math.*   13. ———— ————

14. "I'm also a graduate of North Island (1) *College* (2) *college,*" (3) *She* (4) *she* added.   14. ———— ————

15. The pastor of St. Paul's Anglican (1) *Church* (2) *church* is an (3) *Australian*
    (4) *australian.*   15. ———— ————

16. Vera disagreed with the review of (1) *The* (2) *the* Heidi Chronicles in (3) *The* (4) *the*
    Vancouver Sun.   16. ———— ————

17. The club (1) *Secretary* (2) *secretary* said that the minutes of the meeting were "
    (3) *Almost* (4) *almost* complete."   17. ———— ————

18. The (1) *Girl Scout* (2) *girl scout* leader pointed out the (3) *Milky Way* (4) *milky way*
    to her troop.   18. ———— ————

19. First–year composition students are required to purchase *Writing* (1) *For* (2) *for*
    Audience (3) *And* (4) *and* Purpose.   19. ———— ————

20. The Counselling Office is in (1) *Room* (2) *room* 4 of Cornet (3) *Hall* (4) *hall.*   20. ———— ————

65. MECHANICS: NUMBERS AND ABBREVIATIONS

(Study Sections 65–67, Numbers, and 68–69, Abbreviations.)

Write the number of the **correct** choice.

Example: That book is (1) *3* (2) *three* days overdue.   <u>2</u>

1. (1) *1971* (2) *The year 1971* will be remembered as a turbulent time in Canada.   1. _____

2. Several American states have raised the drinking age to (1) *twenty-one* (2) *21.*   2. _____

3. (1) *Prof.* (2) *Professor* Hilton teaches Asian philosophy.   3. _____

4. Mr. Mulroney was born in (1) *Que.* (2) *Quebec.*   4. _____

5. Why is there no (1) *thirteenth* (2) *13th* floor in this building?   5. _____

6. The exam will be held at noon on (1) *Fri.* (2) *Friday.*   6. _____

7. The (1) *P.O.* (2) *post office* on campus always has a long line of international students sending letters and packages to their families and friends.   7. _____

8. He worked for the Creighton (1) *Company* (2) *Co.* for ten years.   8. _____

9. Nicole will study in Germany, (1) *Eng.* (2) *England,* and Sweden next year.   9. _____

10. Robert Bailey, (1) *M.D.* (2) *medical doctor,* is my physician.   10. _____

11. What is 22 feet, (1) *3* (2) *three* inches in metric?   11. _____

12. For the lab, the department purchased markers, pads of paper, (1) *etc.,* (2) *and other office supplies.*   12. _____

13. For (1) *Xmas* (2) *Christmas,* the Fords planned a quiet family gathering.   13. _____

14. It was necessary for him to leave the campus by 2 (1) *p.m.* (2) *o'clock.*   14. _____

15. John's stipend was (1) *$2,145* (2) *two thousand, one hundred, forty-five dollars.*   15. _____

16. She will graduate from medical school June (1) *2* (2) *second,* 1998.   16. _____

17. He and his family moved to Sooke last (1) *Feb.* (2) *February,* didn't they?   17. _____

18. Over (1) *900* (2) *nine hundred* students attend Hillcrest Junior High School.   18. _____

19. He detested his early normal (1) *phys. ed.* (2) *physical education* class.   19. _____

20. Next year's convention will be held on April (1) *19* (2)*19th,* (3) *nineteenth,* in Burlington.   20. _____

21. The petition contained (1) *2,983* (2) *two thousand, nine hundred, eighty-three* names.   21. _____

22. The lottery prize has reached an colossal (1) *ten million dollars* (2) *$10 million.*   22. _____

23. Our neighbour had adopted a (1) *two-month-old* (2) *2-month-old* baby boy.   23. _____

24. (1) *The Reverend Harold Olson* (2) *Rev. Olson* was the speaker.   24. _____

25. The diagram was on (1) *pg.* (2) *page* 44.   25. _____

26. Mrs. Latimer will teach (1) *English* (2) *Eng.* next semester at Stelly High School.   26. _____

27. Jody bought a puppy at the SPCA for (1) *Xmas* (2) *Christmas.*   27. _____

28. Jack's dissertation was (1) *two hundred fifty* (2) *250 pages.*   28. _____

29. The plane expected from (1) *B.C early this a.m* (2) *British Columbia early this morning* is late. 29. _____

30. The bus arrives at 10:55 a.m. and leaves at (1) *11:00* (2) *eleven* a.m. 30. _____

31. Ben earned (1) *three hundred dollars* (2) *$300,* saved $80, and spent the rest on books and movies. 31. _____

32. Rachel's name was (1) *twenty-sixth* (2) *26th* on the list of high school graduates. 32. _____

33. The bad roads meant I had to use (1) *4-* (2) *four-*wheel drive. 33. _____

66. MECHANICS: CAPITALS, NUMBERS, AND ABBREVIATIONS

(Study Sections 61–63, Capitalization; 65–67, Numbers; and 68–69, Abbreviations.)

In the first column, write the number of the **first correct** choice (**1** or **2**).
In the second column, write the number of the **second correct** choice (**3** or **4**).

Example: There are only (1) *three* (2) *3* more days until (3) *Summer* (4) *summer* vacation.   _1_ _4_

1. Racial attitudes of many South African (1) *White* (2) *white* people will be challenged as all citizens are guaranteed their (3) *Civil Rights* (4) *civil rights.*   1. ____ ____

2. We have an (1) *Aboriginal* (2) *aboriginal* from Pond Inlet studying (3) *Engineering* (4) *engineering* here.   2. ____ ____

3. My (1) *Supervisor* (2) *supervisor* said our report was (3) *"Super!"* (4) *"super!"*   3. ____ ____

4. "I expect," he said, (1) *To* (2) *to* get an *A* in my (3) *Chem.* (4) *chemistry* class.   4. ____ ____

5. On June (1) *6* (2) *6th,* 1982, she spoke at Loyola (3) *High School* (4) *high school.*   5. ____ ____

6. The new college (1) *President* (2) *president* greeted the (3) *Alumni* (4) *alumni.*   6. ____ ____

7. A (1) *canadian* (2) *Canadian* flag flies from the top of the Customs (3) *building* (4) *Building.*   7. ____ ____

8. The (1) *treasurer* (2) *Treasurer* of the (3) *Junior Accountants Club* (4) *junior accountants club* has absconded with our dues.   8. ____ ____

9. (1) *308* (2) *Three hundred eight* students passed the test, out of (3) *427* (4) *four hundred twenty-seven* who took it.   9. ____ ____

10. She likes her (1) *english* (2) *English* and (3) *science* (4) *Science* classes.   10. ____ ____

11. Every British Columbian knows that (1) *fall* (2) *Fall* means rain, rain, and more rain for Vancouver (3) *Island* (4) *island.*   11. ____ ____

12. Industry in the (1) *West* (2) *west* is described in this month's (3) *Canadian Business* (4) *Canadian business* magazine.   12. ____ ____

13. Polly is going to take an (1) *english* (2) *English* course this semester instead of one in (3) *History* (4) *history.*   13. ____ ____

14. She was happy; (1) *She* (2) *she* had reservations on (3) *Canadian airlines* (4) *Canadian Airlines.*   14. ____ ____

15. The new (1) *doctor* (2) *Doctor* has opened an office on Fort (3) *Street* (4) *street.*   15. ____ ____

16. The (1) *chinese* (2) *Chinese* students have planned their (3) *3rd* (4) *third* annual Asian festival.   16. ____ ____

17. I spent (1) *New Year's Day* (2) *new year's day* with (3) *mother* (4) *Mother.*   17. ____ ____

18. Her (1) *French* (2) *french* teacher is going to the (3) *Orient* (4) *orient.*   18. ____ ____

19. I need a (1) *Psychology* (2) *psychology* book from the (3) *Library* (4) *library.*   19. ____ ____

20. The (1) *class* (2) *Class* of '75 honoured the (3) *Dean of Law* (4) *dean of law.*   20. ____ ____

21. Carla enrolled in (1) *Doctor* (2) *Dr.* Newell's history course; she is majoring in (3) *social science* (4) *Social Science.*   21. ____ ____

22. Jim moved to eastern Ontario; (1) *He* (2) *he* bought over (3) *400* (4) *four hundred* milking cows.

22. _____ _____

23. She knows (1) *four* (2) *4* students who are going to (3) *College* (4) *college* this fall.

23. _____ _____

24. The (1) *Conservative* (2) *conservative* Prime Minister appointed several former colleague to the (3) *Senate* (4) *senate.*

24. _____ _____

25. Many (1) *italian* (2) *Italians* immigrated to this (3) *country* (4) *Country* after World War II.

25. _____ _____

67. SPELLING: RECOGNIZING CORRECT FORMS

(Study Sections 70–73, Spelling.)

Write the number of the **correctly spelled** word.

Example: A knowledge of (1) *grammar* (2) *grammer* is helpful.   1. __1__

1. (1) *Athletics* (2) *Atheletics* can be both healthful and enjoyable.   1. _____

2. Glenn hopes to add (1) *playright* (2) *playwright* to his list of professional credentials.   2. _____

3. No one thought that a romance would (1) *develope* (2) *develop* between those two.   3. _____

4. Mrs. Smith will not (1) *acknowlege* (2) *acknowledge* whether she received the check.   4. _____

5. I was hoping for a (1) *surprise* (2) *surprize*.   5. _____

6. The children were taught to be (1) *courtous* (2) *courteous* to adults.   6. _____

7. One of the volunteers will be (1) *ninety* (2) *ninty* years old next week.   7. _____

8. The salary will depend on how (1) *competant* (2) *competent* the employee is.   8. _____

9. I loved listening to Grandpa's tales about his childhood because he always (1) *ecsaggerated* (2) *exaggerated* the details.   9. _____

10. It's too bad that Dan always reacted so negatively to (1) *criticism* (2) *critcism*.   10. _____

11. He offered several (1) *ridiculous* (2) *rediculous* excuses for his behaviour.   11. _____

12. (1) *Approximately* (2) *Approximatly* fifty families attended the adoption support group meeting.   12. _____

13. The murder was a (1) *tradegy* (2) *tragedy* felt by the entire community.   13. _____

14. I could not remember the definition of (1) *nucleus* (2) *nuclious*.   14. _____

15. Everyone could hear the (1) *argument* (2) *arguement* between the two young lovers.   15. _____

16. Tim asked a number of questions in class because he was not sure what the professor (1) *ment* (2) *meant* by a "term paper of reasonable length."   16. _____

17. The (1) *ommission* (2) *omission* of the professor's name on the student's article caused an uproar in the department.   17. _____

18. Carrying public liability insurance is a (1) *necessary* (2) *neccessary* condition of registering a car.   18. _____

19. The older generation preferred to (1) *reminisce* (2) *reminice* at the reunion rather than to hike in the woods or swim in the lake.   19. _____

20. Meeting with a tutor for an hour before the examination was a (1) *desperate* (2) *desparate* attempt by Tom to pass his math class.   20. _____

21. Dave was upset about his pitching in the (1) *nineth* (2) *ninth* inning.   21. _____

22. Sally needed a lot of (1) *repetition* (2) *repitition* in order to memorize the formulas for her next chemistry test.   22. _____

23. How (1) *definite* (2) *defenite* is the date for the party?   23. _____

24. Unfortunately, we could not find the written (1) *guarantee* (2) *garantee* when our new television stopped working.   24. _____

25. Jake worked hard because he hoped his temporary job would eventually become a (1) *permenent* (2) *permanent* position.   25. _____

26. I always bring back a (1) *souvenir* (2) *suvinir* for my family when I travel on business.   26. _____

27. We were glad that the (1) *auxilary* (2) *auxiliary* lights came on during the severe thunderstorm.   27. _____

28. Rodney, unfortunately, had not (1) *fulfilled* (2) *fullfilled* the requirements for graduation.   28. _____

29. In our school, students in the (1) *twelth* (2) *twelfth* grade must pass a basic skills test before they may graduate.   29. _____

30. This year, our five-year-old son began to question the (1) *existance* (2) *existence* of the tooth fairy.   30. _____

31. When Harold turned (1) *forty* (2) *fourty,* his office mates filled his office with black balloons and threw him a surprise party.   31. _____

32. Alexi said that one of the worst aspects of life in the former Soviet Union was the (1) *suppression* (2) *suppresion* of religious activity.   32. _____

33. Jack (1) *use to* (2) *used to* rewrite his biology notes.   33. _____

34. I was sitting in my room when the incident (1) *occured* (2) *occurred* in the lobby.   34. _____

35. Perhaps as we grow older, we forget the pain and pressures of our (1) *adolescence* (2) *adolesence.*   35. _____

36. The (1) *phychologist* (2) *psychologist* arranged a group therapy program for procrastinators.   36. _____

37. The arbitrator's solution seemed (1) *sensible* (2) *sensable.*   37. _____

38. We had better (1) *allot* (2) *alot* more resources.   38. _____

39. An (1) *erroneous* (2) *erronous* announcement appeared in the local newspaper.   39. _____

40. The high school's star athlete was a very (1) *conscientous* (2) *conscientious* student.   40. _____

41. The (1) *rythm* (2) *rhythm* of the song seemed to pound in his soul.   41. _____

42. The (1) *heigth* (2) *height* of the boxer intimidated his opponent.   42. _____

43. Filling out (1) *questionaires* (2) *questionnaires* proved to be very time-consuming.   43. _____

44. Lepage's (1) *perseverance* (2) *perseverence* led to his ultimate success in the theatre.   44. _____

45. She has a (1) *tendancy* (2) *tendency* to do her best work early in the day.   45. _____

46. Her services had become (1) *indispensible* (2) *indispensable* to the firm.   46. _____

47. A reception was held for students having an (1) *excellent* (2) *excellant* scholastic record.   47. _____

48. Steven patiently explained the (1) *mathamatics* (2) *mathematics* of the experiment to me, but I was still lost.   48. _____

49. You will find no (1) *prejudice* (2) *predjudice* in our organization.   49. _____

50. Caldwell is (1) *suppose to* (2) *supposed to* deliver the lumber some time today.   50. _____

68. SPELLING: CORRECTING ERRORS

(Study Sections 70–73, Spelling.)

After each **correct** word, write **1** in the first column and nothing in the second column.
After each **misspelled** word, write **0** in the first column and the correct spelling in the second column.

Example: vacumm   0   vacuum

1. unusualy	1. _____	28. synonim	28. _____
2. oppinion	2. _____	29. catagory	29. _____
3. criticize	3. _____	30. fourty	30. _____
4. definite	4. _____	31. managment	31. _____
5. proceedure	5. _____	32. amateur	32. _____
6. artical	6. _____	33. tendancy	33. _____
7. pursue	7. _____	34. prejudice	34. _____
8. accross	8. _____	35. nineth	35. _____
9. acknowlege	9. _____	36. preform	36. _____
10. maneuver	10. _____	37. excelent	37. _____
11. surprise	11. _____	38. guarantee	38. _____
12. absense	12. _____	39. persistant	39. _____
13. sacrefice	13. _____	40. curiosity	40. _____
14. mischievious	14. _____	41. argument	41. _____
15. prevalent	15. _____	42. exaggerate	42. _____
16. parallel	16. _____	43. knowledge	43. _____
17. auxiliary	17. _____	44. rhythem	44. _____
18. fascinating	18. _____	45. reminise	45. _____
19. indepindent	19. _____	46. eighth	46. _____
20. bussiness	20. _____	47. maintenence	47. _____
21. acquire	21. _____	48. existance	48. _____
22. truely	22. _____	49. playwright	49. _____
23. repetition	23. _____	50. doesn't	50. _____
24. apologize	24. _____		
25. adolescense	25. _____		
26. sincereley	26. _____		
27. nucleus	27. _____		

69. SPELLING: CORRECTING ERRORS

(Study Sections 70–73, Spelling.)

On each line, **one** of the three words is misspelled.
In the first blank, write the column number of the **misspelled** word.
In the second blank, write the misspelled word **correctly.**

Column 1	Column 2	Column 3	Column Number	Correct Spelling
Example: definate	opinion	already	1	definite
1. prevalent	guarantee	perserverence	1. _____	_____
2. forty	discription	procedure	2. _____	_____
3. criticism	tradegy	fulfill	3. _____	_____
4. exagerate	suppression	used to	4. _____	_____
5. acquired	pursue	auxillary	5. _____	_____
6. acknowledge	truely	unusually	6. _____	_____
7. apparant	maneuver	parallel	7. _____	_____
8. ryhthm	restaurant	psychology	8. _____	_____
9. sensible	dosn't	maintenance	9. _____	_____
10. ninty	ninth	twelfth	10. _____	_____
11. argument	curiousity	secretary	11. _____	_____
12. sensable	erroneous	meant	12. _____	_____
13. schedule	tendency	questionaire	13. _____	_____
14. nucleus	sacrefice	mischievous	14. _____	_____
15. accross	playwright	perform	15. _____	_____
16. guidance	ommission	independent	16. _____	_____
17. fasinating	opportunity	reminisce	17. _____	_____
18. hindrance	erroneous	hypocricy	18. _____	_____
19. catagory	acquaintance	management	19. _____	_____
20. existance	eighth	courteous	20. _____	_____
21. synonym	mathamatics	particularly	21. _____	_____
22. vacuum	suvenir	supposed to	22. _____	_____
23. definite	neccessary	repetition	23. _____	_____
24. permanant	condemn	business	24. _____	_____
25. meant	surprize	sophomore	25. _____	_____
26. analisis	criticize	excellent	26. _____	_____

27. prejudise   persistent   adolescence   27. _____   _____

28. irrelevent   conscientious   approximately   28. _____   _____

29. irresistible   knowlege   height   29. _____   _____

30. article   develope   ridiculous   30. _____   _____

31. permissable   calendar   apologize   31. _____   _____

32. schedule   sincerly   absence   32. _____   _____

33. commitee   desperate   discipline   33. _____   _____

70. SPELLING: WORDS FREQUENTLY MISSPELLED

(Study Sections 70–73, Spelling.)

In the numbered blank, write the number of the **letter missing** in the word:
1 for **a, 2** for **e, 3** for **i, 4** for **o.** If **no letter is missing,** write **0.**

Example: gramm r   __1__

1. suppr ssion   1. _____
2. tend ncy   2. _____
3. nin ty   3. _____
4. nucl us   4. _____
5. defin te   5. _____
6. permiss ble   6. _____
7. perm nent   7. _____
8. guid nce   8. _____
9. d scription   9. _____
10. fascinat ing   10. _____
11. gu rantee   11. _____
12. abs nce   12. _____
13. appar nt   13. _____
14. hindr nce   14. _____
15. crit cism   15. _____
16. develop_   16. _____
17. indispens ble   17. _____
18. am teur   18. _____
19. argu ment   19. _____
20. me nt   20. _____

21. math matics   21. _____
22. pre judice   22. _____
23. par llel   23. _____
24. sens ble   24. _____
25. prev lent   25. _____
26. rest urant   26. _____
27. rep tition   27. _____
28. nec ssary   28. _____
29. sacr fice   29. _____
30. compet nt   30. _____
31. desp rate   31. _____
32. tru ly   32. _____
33. exist nce   33. _____
34. excell nt   34. _____
35. surpr se   35. _____
36. independ nt   36. _____
37. irresist ble   37. _____
38. persever nce   38. _____
39. opp rtunity   39. _____
40. acknowl dge   40. _____

In the numbered blank,
write **1** if the mising letters are **ie**;
write **2** if the missing letters are **ei**.

1. h r   1. _____   6. v n   6. _____
2. ach ve   2. _____   7. ch f   7. _____
3. dec ve   3. _____   8. l sure   8. _____
4. c ling   4. _____   9. th r   9. _____
5. w rd   5. _____   10. w gh   10. _____

71. USAGE: WORDS SIMILAR IN SOUND

(Study Section 80, The Right Word.)

Write the number of the **correct** choice.

Example: (1) *Your* (2) *You're* lovelier than ever.   2

1. Take my (1) *advice* (2) *advise,* Jake; stay home today.   1. _____

2. The contract was (1) *alright* (2) *all right* until one of the partners began to steal from the company.   2. _____

3. If you (1) *break* (2) *brake* the car gently, you won't feel a jolt.   3. _____

4. Camping trailers with (1) *canvas* (2) *canvass* tops are cooler than hardtop trailers.   4. _____

5. The diamond tiara stolen from the museum exhibit weighed more than three (1) *carets.* (2) *carats.*   5. _____

6. The Dean of Students doubted whether the young man was a (1) *credible* (2) *creditable* witness
   to the fire in the residence.   6. _____

7. The sandpaper was too (1) *course* (2) *coarse* for the job.   7. _____

8. Helping Allan with history was quite a (1) *decent* (2) *descent* gesture, don't you agree?   8. _____

9. This little (1) *device* (2) *devise* will revolutionize the computer industry.   9. _____

10. The professor made an (1) *allusion* (2) *illusion* to a recent disaster in Jerusalem when
    describing crowd behavior.   10. _____

11. We (1) *respectfully* (2) *respectively* request your help at the meeting.   11. _____

12. She was one of the most (1) *imminent* (2) *eminent* educators of the decade.   12. _____

13. We knew that enemy troops would try to (1) *envelop* (2) *envelope* us.   13. _____

14. Jimmy (1) *formerly* (2) *formally* had pitched for the Jays.   14. _____

15. Go (1) *fourth* (2) *forth,* graduates, and be happy as well as successful.   15. _____

16. Despite their obvious differences, the five students in Suite 401A had developed a real
    friendship (1) *among* (2) *between* themselves.   16. _____

17. The software game created by Frank really was (1) *ingenious* (2) *ingenuous.*   17. _____

18. The ferry made the trip to the (1) *aisle* (2) *isle* in less than an hour.   18. _____

19. She tried vainly to (1) *lessen* (2) *lesson* the tension in the house.   19. _____

20. The mourners wept as they filed (1) *passed* (2) *past* the family.   20. _____

21. The style of furniture is actually a matter of (1) *personal* (2) *personnel* taste.   21. _____

22. Even though Gary studied hard and attended every class, he discovered that he was
    (1) *disinterested* (2) *uninterested* in science.   22. _____

23. The Queen's (1) *presents* (2) *presence* always adds special importance to an occasion.   23. _____

24. When the grand marshal gave the signal, the parade (1) *preceded.* (2) *proceeded.*   24. _____

25. Middle-aged professionals are forsaking their high-powered life-style for a (1) *quiet* (2) *quite*
    existence in the country.   25. _____

26. (1) *Weather* (2) *Whether* to pay off all her creditors was a big question to be resolved.   26. _____

27. You can buy typing paper at any (1) *stationary* (2) *stationery* store.   27. _____

28. They knew better (1) *than* (2) *then* we did what the answer was.   28. _____

29. The insult went (1) *thorough* (2) *through* me like a sharp knife.   29. _____

30. Passing doctoral qualifying exams is essentially a (1) *rite* (2) *right* of passage.   30. _____

31. She is the first (1) *woman* (2) *women* to umpire in this league.   31. _____

32. (1) *Your* (2) *You're* aware, aren't you, that the play is sold out?   32. _____

33. This laser printer will (1) *complement* (2) *compliment* your computer.   33. _____

72. USAGE: WORDS SIMILAR IN SOUND

(Study Section 80, The Right Word.)

Write the number of the **correct** choice.

Example: William is (1) *to* (2) *too* clever for his own good.   _2_

1. The rulers of the planet Zircon will (1) *advice* (2) *advise* Earthlings not to land there.   1. _____
2. She signed the letter, "(1) *Respectively* (2) *Respectfully* Yours."   2. _____
3. The student was (1) *anxious* (2) *eager* to receive his award at the banquet.   3. _____
4. These graphs should (1) *complement* (2) *compliment* your written report perfectly.   4. _____
5. "Go (1) *forth* (2) *fourth* and sell those popcorn balls!" shouted the enthusiastic Boy Scout leader.   5. _____
6. Kim should be careful not to (1) *lose* (2) *loose* his temper.   6. _____
7. It's bigger (1) *than* (2) *then* ever!   7. _____
8. The salesperson wrote a memo (1) *in regard to* (2) *in regards to* the drastic change in sales.   8. _____
9. Knowing that they have sufficient funds will (1) *lessen* (2) *lesson* their financial worries.   9. _____
10. The spectators fled when Marshall picked up the (1) *discus* (2) *discuss.*   10. _____
11. Nobody (1) *accept* (2) *except* Gloria would stoop so low.   11. _____
12. Sam unplugged his phone, locked his door, and worked (1) *continuously* (2) *continually* on his research paper.   12. _____
13. You will not find a better (1) *woman* (2) *women* in the department.   13. _____
14. Her approach for preparing for the history final was (1) *different from* (2) *different than* my strategy.   14. _____
15. (1) *Everyone* (2) *Every one* of the disks was destroyed by the flood.   15. _____
16. If he (1) *past* (2) *passed* the physics test, it must be easy.   16. _____
17. Brian Mulroney (1) *preceded* (2) *proceeded* Jean Chretien as Prime Minister.   17. _____
18. The library copy of the magazine had lost (1) *its* (2) *it's* cover.   18. _____
19. He made his way (1) *thorough* (2) *through* the heavy underbrush.   19. _____
20. The royal couple (1) *already* (2) *all ready* is realizing that their marriage may be in trouble.   20. _____
21. Can you name the (1) *capitals* (2) *capitols* of the ten provinces of Canada?   21. _____
22. The committee, unfortunately, may have misunderstood (1) *your* (2) *you're* intentions.   22. _____
23. His physical condition showed the (1) *affects* (2) *effects* of inadequate rest and diet.   23. _____
24. (1) *Irregardless* (2) *Regardless* of the weather, I plan to drive to Whistler this weekend.   24. _____
25. The country was (1) *quiet* (2) *quite* displeased by the diplomat's insensitivity to cultural differences.   25. _____
26. The steep (1) *descent* (2) *decent* down the mountain road was very hazardous.   26. _____
27. They all dressed (1) *formally* (2) *formerly* for the charity ball.   27. _____

28. To be an effective teacher had become her (1) *principal* (2) *principle* concern. 28. _____

29. Are you certain that the bracelet is made of ten-(1) *carat* (2) *carrot* gold? 29. _____

30. The Farkle family were (1) *altogether* (2) *all together* in the living room when their good friend and trusted neighbour made his announcement. 30. _____

31. The student (1) *inferred* (2) *implied* from the professor that the test would be hard. 31. _____

32. If Sam (1) *had* (2) *would have* attended class more often, he would have passed the first examination. 32. _____

33. "I, (1) *to* (2) *too* (3) *two,* have a statement to make," she said. 33. _____

34. Poverty—(1) *its* (2) *it's* no longer just a Third World problem. 34. _____

35. Chris feels (1) *good* (2) *well* now that she received an allergy shot. 35. _____

36. He said, "(1) *Their* (2) *There* (3) *They're* is no reason for you to wait." 36. _____

37. The writer (1) *inferred* (2) *implied* that most people know little of international politics. 37. _____

38. "(1) *Whose* (2) *Who's* there?" she whispered hoarsely. 38. _____

39. The cat ran behind my car, and I accidentally drove over (1) *its* (2) *it's* tail. 39. _____

40. Gary's report will (1) *ensure* (2) *insure* more funding. 40. _____

41. Many employees feel that their decision to smoke at home is a (1) *personal* (2) *personnel* decision and not the company's to make. 41. _____

42. The twins (1) *formally* (2) *formerly* attended a community college in Ontario. 42. _____

43. The mere (1) *cite* (2) *sight* (3) *site* of Julia made his heart soar. 43. _____

44. I hope to install a (1) *device* (2) *devise* that will serve as a burglar alarm. 44. _____

45. (1) *Hopefully* (2) *We hope that* the instructor will post our grades before we leave for the holidays. 45. _____

46. The players absolutely rejected the (1) *principal* (2) *principle* of a salary cap. 46. _____

47. The comic's act was vulgar and his manners (1) *coarse* (2) *course.* 47. _____

48. If North Americans realized that secondary smoke causes over three thousand lung-cancer deaths each year, (1) *than* (2) *then* perhaps fewer parents would smoke around their children. 48. _____

49. Will people be standing in the (1) *aisles* (2) *isles* at the dedication ceremony? 49. _____

50. Dr. Smith is (1) *famous* (2) *notable* for her educational research. 50. _____

51. "Sad movies always (1) *affect* (2) *effect* me this way." 51. _____

52. She could not decide (1) *weather* (2) *whether* or not to go back to work. 52. _____

53. The president suggested a (1) *canvas* (2) *canvass* of the members of the organization. 53. _____

54. He was obviously (1) *effected* (2) *affected* by the beauty of his surroundings. 54. _____

55. Even after several proofreadings, the new (1) *stationary* (2) *stationery* had several errors in the address. 55. _____

56. John decided to change the oil in the car (1) *himself* (2) *hisself.* 56. _____

57. He is very (1) *thorough* (2) *through* and painstaking in all that he does. 57. _____

58. Jonathan had the (1) *presence* (2) *presents* of mind to make a sharp right turn and step on the accelerator. 58. _____

59. (1) *These* (2) *This* door needs repair before the weekend guests arrive. 59. _____

60. This biology textbook has a (1) *most unique* (2) *unique* front cover design. 60. _____

61. The findings of our committee (1) **correspond to** (2) **correspond with** the responses from the student questionnaire. 61. _____

62. Dr. Pechter is a distinguished and (1) **eminent** (2) **imminent** member of the faculty. 62. _____

63. The children were (1) **already** (2) **all ready** for this trip. 63. _____

64. The teacher had reported the matter to the (1) **principal** (2) **principle.** 64. _____

65. It's obvious that (1) **their** (2) **there** (3) **they're** unwilling to listen to reason. 65. _____

66. The professor was (1) **angry** (2) **mad** because the students slept during the lecture. 66. _____

67. An (1) **individual** (2) **person** dropped off a package at the mailroom. 67. _____

68. The track coach told me that he wanted to (1) **discus** (2) **discuss** my performance at the last meet. 68. _____

69. The moving object had now become (1) **stationary** (2) **stationery.** 69. _____

70. "What is (1) **your** (2) **you're** candid opinion?" she asked. 70. _____

71. (1) **Who's** (2) **Whose** theory do you believe regarding the geographical origin of humankind? 71. _____

72. In the mountains, we quickly felt the (1) **affects** (2) **effects** of a change in elevation. 72. _____

73. We suspected that an upset in our plans was (1) **eminent** (2) **imminent.** 73. _____

74. Even with all their sophisticated research instrumentation, the anthropologists weren't (1) **quiet** (2) **quite** sure of the origin and age of the skull. 74. _____

75. In later life, Toto was appointed honourary (1) **counsel** (2) **council** (3) **consul** for the Land of Oz. 75. _____

73. USAGE

(Study Section 80, The Right Word.)

Write the number of the **correct** choice.
(Formal nonsexist usage is intended.)

Example: Willa wanted the doll very (1) *much* (2) *badly.*   1. __1__

1. Your essay has (1) *its* (2) *it's* faults, but it makes some excellent points too.   1. _____

2. A tall tree has fallen and is (1) *laying* (2) *lying* across the highway.   2. _____

3. A (1) *percent* (2) *percentage* of the solution evaporated.   3. _____

4. Tragically, the wrong man was (1) *hung* (2) *hanged.*   4. _____

5. Did you ask if he will (1) *let* (2) *leave* you open a charge account?   5. _____

6. She thought that she had paid (1) *to* (2) *too* (3) *two* much for her television set.   6. _____

7. Becca discovered that her backpack had (1) *burst* (2) *bursted* (3) *busted* because she was carrying too many books.   7. _____

8. We were surprised (1) *somewhat* (2) *some* at his sudden outburst.   8. _____

9. The old inn (1) *used* (2) *utilized* a local bakery for the dessert menu.   9. _____

10. Will the new legislation (1) *affect* (2) *effect* your business enterprise?   10. _____

11. The owner (1) *accepted* (2) *excepted* the resignation of the general manager.   11. _____

12. We were (1) *real* (2) *very* pleased that they came to the rodeo.   12. _____

13. Michael and you will have to share the book (1) *between* (2) *among* you.   13. _____

14. We heard the same report (1) *everywhere* (2) *everywheres* we traveled.   14. _____

15. I knew that it would be (1) *alright* (2) *all right* for us to travel overseas.   15. _____

16. That the people are sovereign is the first (1) *principal* (2) *principle* of a democratic society.   16. _____

17. As soon as he had (1) *affected* (2) *effected* his release, he telephoned her.   17. _____

18. Do (1) *try to* (2) *try and* spend the night with us when you are in town.   18. _____

19. I suspected that Sue's mother was (1) *most* (2) *almost* at the end of her patience.   19. _____

20. Shooting innocent bystanders is one of the most (1) *amoral* (2) *immoral* street crimes committed.   20. _____

21. The alfalfa milkshake may taste awful, but it is (1) *healthy* (2) *healthful.*   21. _____

22. The tennis player always (1) *lays* (2) *lies* down before an important match.   22. _____

23. Timothy (1) *lay* (2) *laid* new linoleum on the floor of the recreation hall.   23. _____

24. Unfortunately, Jack is often (1) *compared to* (2) *compared with* his older brother.   24. _____

25. When our neighbours' dog wants (1) *in* (2) *to come in* our yard, she stands up on her hind feet and peers over the fence.   25. _____

26. The (1) *amount* (2) *number* of trees needed to produce a single book should humble any author.   26. _____

27. We were (1) *altogether* (2) *all together* satisfied with the arrangements.   27. _____

28. The Allies' scheme was (1) **practicable** (2) **practical** but dangerous. 28. _____

29. I (1) **had ought** (2) **ought** to have let her know the time of my arrival. 29. _____

30. They had (1) **already** (2) **all ready** canceled their reservations. 30. _____

31. The newspaper was soggy because it had (1) **laid** (2) **lain** in a rain puddle all morning. 31. _____

32. After spending $1,000 on repairs, we hope that the van finally works (1) **like** (2) **as** it should. 32. _____

33. The couple (1) **adapted** (2) **adopted** a baby girl from Bulgaria. 33. _____

34. Will you be sure to (1) **contact** (2) **get in touch with** me tomorrow? 34. _____

35. He (1) **seldom ever** (2) **hardly ever** writes to his sister. 35. _____

36. Cindy was (1) **besides** (2) **beside** herself with anger. 36. _____

37. Jeff is pitching (1) **good** (2) **well** this spring. 37. _____

38. Do not (1) **set** (2) **sit** the floppy disk on top of the computer monitor. 38. _____

39. The play was from (1) **classical** (2) **classic** Rome. 39. _____

40. One reason for his poor health is (1) **because** (2) **that** he doesn't get enough sleep. 40. _____

41. The curtain was about to (1) **raise** (2) **rise** on the last act of the boring play. 41. _____

42. She lived in constant fear of (1) **losing** (2) **loosing** her passport. 42. _____

43. The customer was (1) **sure** (2) **surely** upset when she discovered that the warranty did not cover the repair. 43. _____

44. Exhausted from their cold plunge into the ocean, the swimmers were (1) **laying** (2) **lying** on the beach. 44. _____

45. The camp is just a few miles (1) **further** (2) **farther** along the trail. 45. _____

46. I wrote to the registrar (1) **in regard to** (2) **in regards to** my missing transcript. 46. _____

47. The passengers were instructed to fasten (1) **they're** (2) **their** (3) **there** seat belts. 47. _____

48. The dictator was (1) **hanged** (2) **hung** immediately after the trial. 48. _____

49. She wanted (1) **badly** (2) **very much** to stay in Japan for a week of sightseeing. 49. _____

50. Lionel was (1) **angry at** (2) **angry with** his mother because she refused to help him buy a car. 50. _____

74. USAGE

(Study Section 80, The Right Word.)

Write **1** if the boldface expression is **correct.**
Write **0** if it is **incorrect.**
(Formal nonsexist usage is intended.)

Example: The car's fender was dented
and ***it's*** windshield was cracked.　　0

1. ***Those sort*** of books are expensive.　1. _____

2. He played ***like*** he was inspired.　2. _____

3. Standards of living have ***raised.***　3. _____

4. Some dogs look ***like*** their masters.　4. _____

5. You ***hadn't ought*** to sneak into the show. 5. _____

6. ***It's*** time for class.　6. _____

7. You ***too*** can afford such a car.　7. _____

8. We were ***plenty*** surprised at the
outcome.　8. _____

9. ***All*** of the books were the wrong
edition.　9. _____

10. He studied ***alot*** for the biology lab
exam.　10. _____

11. The cornerstone was being ***laid.***　11. _____

12. ***Irregardless*** of the result, you did
your best.　12. _____

13. Will he ***raise*** your salary?　13. _____

14. Try to keep him ***off of*** the pier.　14. _____

15. I ***always*** read to my children.　15. _____

16. His ***presence*** was required.　16. _____

17. His efforts at improving his math skills
are ***creditable.***　17. _____

18. Her success was ***due to*** hard work
and persistence.　18. _____

19. I'm to go too, ***aren't I?***　19. _____

20. ***They're*** house is now for sale.　20. _____

21. Henry and ***myself*** decided to start a
small business together.　21. _____

22. The club has lost ***its*** president.　22. _____

23. Susan is ***awfully*** depressed.　23. _____

24. Did he ***lay*** awake last night?　24. _____

25. The professor's opinion about the
difficulty level of the test ***differed
with*** the teaching assistant's
impression.　25. _____

26. Bob ***laid*** the carpet in the hallway.　26. _____

27. We ***sure*** hope you are able to go.　27. _____

28. He ***better*** get here before noon.　28. _____

29. She is a ***real*** hard worker.　29. _____

30. The cat ***has been laying*** on top of the
refrigerator all morning.　30. _____

31. I admire ***that kind*** of initiative.　31. _____

32. He has ***plenty*** of opportunities for
earning money.　32. _____

33. He was ***plenty*** worried at not hearing
from her.　33. _____

34. David looked ***like*** he wanted to avoid
her.　34. _____

35. ***Most*** all her friends sent cards.　35. _____

36. The damage was ***nowhere near*** as
great as I thought it might be.　36. _____

37. He always did ***good*** in English.　37. _____

38. She resigned ***because of*** illness.　38. _____

39. The flood seemed ***imminent.***　39. _____

40. Max has ***less*** enemies than Sam.　40. _____

41. The speaker ***inferred*** that success
depended as much on attitude as skill.　41. _____

42. He has a long ***way*** to go tonight.　42. _____

43. Did he ***loose*** his credit cards?　43. _____

44. She walked ***like*** she was in pain.　44. _____

45. Walking to school was a *rite* of passage in our home.

45. _____

46. Who were the *principals* in the company?

46. _____

47. His finances are in bad *shape.*

47. _____

48. Have you written *in regards to* an appointment?

48. _____

49. Elaine *adopted* her novel for television.

49. _____

50. Damp weather *affects* her sinuses.

50. _____

75. USAGE

(Study Section 80, The Right Word.)

Write the number of the **correct** choice.
(Formal nonsexist usage is intended.)

Example: Fix it (1) *anyways* (2) *any way* you can.   <u>2</u>

1. The book's author was (1) *censored* (2) *censured* for his views.   1. ——————

2. You may borrow (1) *any one* (2) *anyone* of my books if you promise to return it.   2. ——————

3. Compared (1) *to* (2) *with* the Riders, the Argos have a weaker defense but a stronger offense.   3. ——————

4. The figure of Venus de Milo is an excellent example of (1) *classic* (2) *classical* sculpture.   4. ——————

5. He *should* (1) *of* (2) *have* notified his hostess of his change in plans.   5. ——————

6. The linebacking unit was (1) *composed* (2) *comprised* of Taylor, Marshall, and Burt.   6. ——————

7. Be (1) *sure to* (2) *sure and* review your class notes for the exam.   7. ——————

8. The young researchers considered everything (1) *accept* (2) *except* the truthfulness of their subject.   8. ——————

9. (1) *Irregardless* (2) *Regardless* of difficulties, he will complete the project.   9. ——————

10. The reason that Kay became a doctor was (1) *because* (2) *that* she enjoyed helping people.   10. ——————

11. The referee was completely (1) *uninterested* (2) *disinterested* and completely dedicated.   11. ——————

12. The three children tried to outrun (1) *each other* (2) *one another.*   12. ——————

13. Early rainstorms had (1) *raised* (2) *risen* the level of the lake.   13. ——————

14. (1) *Everyplace* (2) *Everywhere* we went, we encountered hospitable people.   14. ——————

15. I spoke to the agent about (1) *ensuring* (2) *insuring* the cottage.   15. ——————

16. I'm a very sloppy person, (1) *aren't I* (2) *am I not* (3) *ain't I?*   16. ——————

17. We could not ship by air the (1) *number* (2) *amount* of cartons that the company ordered.   17. ——————

18. My history book was (1) *setting* (2) *sitting* in the study carrel, where I had left it.   18. ——————

19. Her brilliant performance was (1) *due to* (2) *because of* talent and ability.   19. ——————

20. Bob and (1) *myself* (2) *I* will spend the summer in the Yukon.   20. ——————

21. Man's first step on the moon was a (1) *historic* (2) *historical* moment in the exploration of space.   21. ——————

22. We had (1) *less* (2) *fewer* problems than we had anticipated.   22. ——————

23. When his pizza arrived, Tom was (1) *nowheres* (2) *nowhere* to be found.   23. ——————

24. The teenagers spent the day (1) *laying* (2) *lying* on the beach in the sun.   24. ——————

25. If you (1) *lose* (2) *loose* your credit card, report the loss at once.   25. ——————

26. He followed directions just (1) *like* (2) *as* he had been instructed.   26. ——————

27. She had a (1) *nice* (2) *agreeable* personality.   27. ——————

28. A (1) *rising* (2) *raising* barometer indicated a marked change in the weather.   28. ——————

29. The house showed the obvious (1) *effects* (2) *affects* of long-term neglect.   29. _____

30. The deep-breathing exercises before the exam (1) *lessoned* (2) *lessened* his test anxiety.   30. _____

31. The new policy will (1) *affect* (2) *effect* who gets a loan.   31. _____

32. The statue (1) *sits* (2) *sets* on a high pedestal opposite the entrance to the park.   32. _____

33. Her former boyfriend walked (1) *past* (2) *passed* without speaking.   33. _____

34. The (1) *site* (2) *cite* for the new library has been selected.   34. _____

35. A cloud of smoke was (1) *rising* (2) *raising* from the distant hillside.   35. _____

36. Detective Chandler gave the apartment a (1) *through* (2) *thorough* inspection.   36. _____

37. The leader's efforts to find them had been (1) *altogether* (2) *all together* praiseworthy.   37. _____

38. People considered him a man of high (1) *principles* (2) *principals.*   38. _____

39. Her attitude toward the problem was quite different (1) *from* (2) *than* his.   39. _____

40. The news (1) *affected* (2) *impacted* Michael in an unexpected manner.   40. _____

41. The newest employee receives (1) *less* (2) *fewer* telephone calls than the rest of the staff.   41. _____

42. She wanted to believe that there was (1) *no such a* (2) *no such* word as *can't.*   42. _____

43. Stan told us an (1) *incredible* (2) *incredulous* story.   43. _____

44. Let the documents (1) *lie* (2) *lay* on the table where he left them.   44. _____

45. The speakers were much better informed about the subject (1) *then* (2) *than* I was.   45. _____

46. His answer was (1) *different than* (2) *different from* mine.   46. _____

47. Please give this form to the (1) *individual* (2) *person* in the next room.   47. _____

48. The politician (1) *to* (2) *too* was in agreement with the remarks made by the student.   48. _____

49. Laurie was (1) *very much* (2) *plenty* upset by her low grade point average for the fall semester.   49. _____

50. He was obviously (1) *two* (2) *to* (3) *too* stunned to speak.   50. _____

76. USAGE

(Study Section 80, The Right Word, and 81, Nonsexist Usage.)

Write **1** if the boldface expression is **correct**.
Write **0** if it is **incorrect**.
(Formal nonsexist usage is intended.)

Example: The day was *like* a bad dream.   _**1**_

1. A lion hunting its prey is *immoral.*   1. _____

2. The bus was *already* to leave.   2. _____

3. The *men* and *girls* on the team played well.   3. _____

4. Has *any one* here seen Betty?   4. _____

5. *Almost* all my friends came.   5. _____

6. The hum of the air conditioner was *continual.*   6. _____

7. The informer is usually *hanged.*   7. _____

8. The air conditioner runs *good* now.   8. _____

9. The child is *too* young to understand.   9. _____

10. *Irregardless* of his shortcomings, she loves him.   10. _____

11. Where is the party *at?*   11. _____

12. He had no intention of jumping *off of* the bridge.   12. _____

13. The vacuum-cleaner *salesman* contacted him.   13. _____

14. The sun will *hopefully* shine tomorrow.   14. _____

15. *They're* financial obligations had become too heavy for them.   15. _____

16. The *workmen* made too much noise with their equipment.   16. _____

17. His chances looked *good.*   17. _____

18. The twins frequently wear *one another's* clothing.   18. _____

19. A twisted branch was *laying* across our path.   19. _____

20. She was *disinterested* in the boring play.   20. _____

21. Send a cover letter to the *chair* of the department.   21. _____

22. The auditorium holds *less* than six hundred people.   22. _____

23. The conflicting groups finally *effected* a compromise.   23. _____

24. The professor was somewhat annoyed at the *girls* in his class.   24. _____

25. Sam *differs from* Gina about the issue of increasing social services.   25. _____

26. I meant to *lay* down for an hour.   26. _____

27. Let's think *further* about it.   27. _____

28. *Hopefully,* it will snow soon.   28. _____

29. He enjoys the *healthy* food we serve.   29. _____

30. The *delusion* that everyone hated him kept Paul from performing well on the job.   30. _____

31. The *husband* and *wife* were both pursuing law degrees.   31. _____

32. Her story was *incredulous.*   32. _____

33. It is a *most unique* situation.   33. _____

34. He had *already* departed.   34. _____

35. Theirs was a *lose* arrangement.   35. _____

36. *Due to* the pollution levels, the city banned incinerators.   36. _____

37. The roommates hollered at *each other* about who had broken the CD player.   37. _____

38. First and second prizes were given to John and Harold, *respectively.*   38. _____

39. Tim was *mad* with love for her.   39. _____

40. Only the *chairman* knew the exact amount in the budget.   40. _____

41. She was **terribly** pleased at winning the contest.

41. _____

42. **Their** is always another game.

42. _____

43. The gold locket had **lain** on the floor of the attic for ten years.

43. _____

44. Let's hope the vote will be sooner rather **then** later.

44. _____

45. Foyt **lead** the race from start to finish.

45. _____

46. By his tone, the news reporter **implied** that the politician was guilty of fraud.

46. _____

47. **Lie** down for a while.

47. _____

48. The cost of living keeps **rising.**

48. _____

49. **They're** not finished with writing the report.

49. _____

50. We ventured **further** into the woods.

50. _____

77. USAGE

(Study Section 80, The Right Word, and 81, Nonsexist Usage.)

Write **1** if the boldface expression is **correct**.
Write **0** if it is **incorrect**.
(Formal nonsexist usage is intended.)

Example: Claire *sure* could sew.   0

1. Two of the rebels were *hanged.*   1. _____

2. The *woman doctor* was quite supportive of her nursing staff.   2. _____

3. She died *due to* pneumonia.   3. _____

4. Jaime *emigrated* from Mexico in 1988.   4. _____

5. The phone rang *continually.*   5. _____

6. The committee decided that the office needed more *manpower* during registration.   6. _____

7. The dig reached the bottom *strata.*   7. _____

8. His reasons for joining the club are different *than* mine.   8. _____

9. *On the basis of the report,* John was promoted.   9. _____

10. *Being as* I was early, I waited.   10. _____

11. He bought chips, soda, *etc.*   11. _____

12. June has *less* days than July.   12. _____

13. Be *sure and* write if you get work.   13. _____

14. He hiked *farther* than I.   14. _____

15. Swimming is *healthful* exercise.   15. _____

16. They *seldom ever* meet.   16. _____

17. There was a *bunch* of people in the waiting room.   17. _____

18. The *aisle* in the small plane was too narrow for my carry-on luggage and me.   18. _____

19. I *set* my packages on the table.   19. _____

20. A *repairman* never seems to arrive on time to scheduled appointments in the home.   20. _____

21. We were *allotted* $15 for refreshments.   21. _____

22. I shall *contact* my attorney.   22. _____

23. John displayed an *ante-intellectual* attitude.   23. _____

24. He fell *off* the ladder.   24. _____

25. I am *nowhere near* ready to go.   25. _____

26. Sue's balloon had *bursted.*   26. _____

27. The temple *sits* on a high hill.   27. _____

28. The children *usually always* bragged about how many toys they had.   28. _____

29. I asked *in regards to* my check.   29. _____

30. She is *apt* to clap her hands when excited.   30. _____

31. *Mankind* needs to seek peaceful solutions to international conflict.   31. _____

32. The *brakes* on the truck should be replaced.   32. _____

33. The *reason* she stutters *is because* she's nervous.   33. _____

34. The blanket was too *coarse* to use on a bed.   34. _____

35. The cat has been *lying* on the hearth all afternoon.   35. _____

36. I'm sure that he will be *O.K.*   36. _____

37. Julie *persuaded* her husband to begin a diet.   37. _____

38. Audrey wrote a *fine* paper.   38. _____

39. She does *well* in examinations.   39. _____

40. The red dress looks *good* on her.   40. _____

41. The psychiatrist was convinced that the defendant was *mad.*   41. _____

42. The students created a mock exam **theirselves.**   42. _____

43. Olsen is a **notable** public enemy.   43. _____

44. I **laid** my driver's license on the counter.   44. _____

45. The class was **all together** bored by the film.   45. _____

46. No modern playwright can be **compared to** Shakespeare.   46. _____

47. All roads lead there. Take **anyone.**   47. _____

48. When offered beer and wine, I choose the **latter.**   48. _____

49. We will **except** you from the rule.   49. _____

50. Is this test **verbal** or written?   50. _____

78. USAGE

(Study Section 80, The Right Word, and 81, Nonsexist Usage.)

Write **1** if the sentence is **correct.**
Write **0** if it is **incorrect;** then correct the error in the second column.
(Formal nonsexist usage is intended.)

Example: Its been a unique experience.	0	It's
1. Some people drive their cars like everyone else on the road was a sworn enemy.	1. ___	_____
2. The interview committee was altogether surprised by the candidate's responses.	2. ___	_____
3. The waitress snarled when I left a quarter for a tip.	3. ___	_____
4. We wanted to lay in the sun for a week and forget about bosses, meetings, memos, and deadlines.	4. ___	_____
5. Being jolted by 50 volts had little apparent affect on Harold, who insisted it had brightened up his day.	5. ___	_____
6. They laid the new floor in the kitchen in less than a day.	6. ___	_____
7. Parker said it was alright with him to put anchovies on the pizza but implied that he was just being polite.	7. ___	_____
8. Irregardless of my grades, I'm an excellent writer, except for word usage.	8. ___	_____
9. Keep your principles and you'll seldom ever regret it.	9. ___	_____
10. She wanted badly to travel to Europe after her graduation from university.	10. ___	_____
11. I sometimes pace around my room when I'm trying to understand a complex thing.	11. ___	_____
12. We were far too credible about the investment, and that's how we lost our capital.	12. ___	_____
13. He better get to class on time; Professor Morrison is apt to complain if he's late again.	13. ___	_____
14. The judge was uninterested; she wished to determine only if the complaint were a genuine instance of discrimination.	14. ___	_____
15. You're absolutely right to go to traffic court and dispute the ticket.	15. ___	_____
16. Providing that she doesn't lose sight of her objective, she's a good bet to make the team.	16. ___	_____
17. When we saw that the restaurant was a little further down the road, our morale greatly improved.	17. ___	_____
18. Lie your head on my shoulder so that you can rest.	18. ___	_____
19. This sort of antivirus program is far more effective than any of the others.	19. ___	_____
20. A policeman should be assigned to patrol the parking lot at night.	20. ___	_____

79. NONSEXIST USAGE

(Study Section 81, Nonsexist Usage.)

Write **1** if the sentence is **correct.**
Write **0** if it is **incorrect;** then correct the error in the second column.
(Formal nonsexist usage is intended.)

Example: The woman scientist is messy around the office.   0   The scientist
_____   _____

1. The male and girl students decided to form separate groups.   1. ___ _____

2. Before the baby was born, I worried about my mothering skills.   2. ___ _____

3. Doctors have increased their interpersonal communication skills.   3. ___ _____

4. Every student must bring his textbook to class.   4. ___ _____

5. The policeman stationed in the parking garage will walk students to their cars. 5. ___ _____

6. The homemakers on our street organized a babysitting cooperative.   6. ___ _____

7. Man's need to survive produces some surprising effects.   7. ___ _____

8. Skaters competing in tournaments often spend five hours a day practicing their routines. 8. ___ _____

9. Girls, it's time to insist that our spouses share in the housework.   9. ___ _____

10. The stewardess spilled coffee on my newspaper.   10. ___ _____

11. A female cement-truck driver delivered the cement for our new driveway.   11. ___ _____

12. The innkeeper and his wife greeted us when we first arrived at the inn.   12. ___ _____

13. The repairman's estimate was much lower than we had expected.   13. ___ _____

14. Everyone hoped that his/her paper would be selected for the award.   14. ___ _____

15. When on an elevator, most people prefer riding in silence.   15. ___ _____

16. The spinster who lives on our street never attends the block parties.   16. ___ _____

17. The male nursing student was certainly a minority in his nursing class.   17. ___ _____

18. The male nurse who helped me after my surgery was a skilled communicator.   18. ___ _____

19. The lady mathematics professor has published several textbooks.   19. ___ _____

20. Mr. Feather's widow is beginning to look for a job outside of the home.   20. ___ _____

80. BEYOND THE SENTENCE: PARAGRAPH DEVELOPMENT WITH SPECIFICS

(Study Section 91, Effective Paragraphs.)

Underline the **topic sentence** in each paragraph. In addition, write **1** in the first blank at the end if the paragraph develops its topic sentence adequately **and** then write another sentence that would continue its development. Write **0** if the paragraph is not adequately developed **and** then write the reason why you think so.

1. Young people today see how their parents feel and act. Since they feel that their parents are wrong, they rebel because they do not want to become carbon copies of their elders. Young people want to be treated as people, not just children who do not know what they are talking about and who should therefore not express their own ideas. Young people today want to do and think as they please. They do not want their ideas to be pushed aside for an older person's ideas. They want a free society where there is nothing that they must do because it is required of them. They want to experience new and different things. Whatever their elders want, they do the opposite so as not to be like them.

1. _____ _____

_____

2. Today's athletes are overpaid. Although it is undeniable that not everyone can toss a basketball through a hoop or throw a baseball ninety miles an hour, that doesn't mean that fans should have to pay the admission prices they do. People who like sports have other ways to spend their money, such as movies or vacations. Some of them can't even afford to go to sporting events. Doctors and nurses also perform valuable services to society; should they be rich enough to retire at thirty-five? The cost of living for the average person continues to climb. Athletes should not be millionaires, no matter how talented they are.

2. _____ _____

_____

3. Provincial governments that propose mandatory exit testing for public high school students should rethink their plans. Many students live stressful lives. Often students must cope with violence in their schools. Some students never know when someone will be seriously injured in their school hallways or classrooms. Just as serious, students must resist the daily temptation of drugs and alcohol. Despite education programs in their neighbourhoods and schools, teenagers remain targets for drug dealers who can infiltrate the playgrounds and classrooms. For some students, home life is no better. Dual-income families or single-parent families force teenagers to fend for themselves after school—no cookies and milk and Mom waiting at home for these students. Educators should be looking for ways to reduce stress in their students' lives—not adding to it.

3. _____ _____

_____

4. The study found that collection crews spent only a small portion of their day picking up garbage. Crews observed in Saanich spent an average of two hours and 55 minutes at it, while those in Oak Bay collected garbage for three hours and 22 minutes a day, and crews in Colwood worked on collection for three hours and 33 minutes a day.

4. _____ _____

_____

_____

5. Multicultural curricula should provide opportunities for all students to explore their own cultures and the cultures of their classmates and communities. Frequently, schools focus on one or two cultures for classroom activities. Students from a British background may feel that they don't have a specific culture to share with their classmates—no special language, clothing, food, or music. Their families' traditions may have been lost over the years or blended with Canada's commercialization of holidays. Multicultural activities should help every child, including those with British roots, to research not only special ceremonies but also everyday expressions of their culture.

5. _____ _____

_____

_____

81. BEYOND THE SENTENCE: PARAGRAPH UNITY

(Study Section 91, Effective Paragraphs.)

Underline the **topic sentence** of each paragraph. Then, in the blank at the end of the paragraph, write the number(s) of any sentence(s) in the paragraph that **do not relate directly** to the topic sentence.

1. [1]From a pebble on the shore to a boulder on a mountainside, any rock you see began as something else and was made a rock by the earth itself. [2]Igneous rock began as lava that over hundreds of years hardened far beneath the earth's surface. [3]Granite is an igneous rock. [4]Sedimentary rock was once sand, mud, or clay that settled to the bottom of a body of water and was packed down in layers under the ocean floor. [5]All rocks are made up of one or more minerals. [6]Metamorphic rock began as either igneous rock or sedimentary rock whose properties were changed by millions of years of exposure to the heat, pressure, and movement below the earth's crust.

1. _____ _____

2. [1]Although we normally associate suits of armor with the knights of medieval Europe, the idea of such protective coverings is much older and more pervasive than that. [2]Some knights even outfitted their horses with metal armor. [3]As long as 3,500 years ago, Assyrian and Babylonian warriors sewed pieces of metal to their leather tunics the better to repel enemy arrows. [4]A thousand years later, the Greeks wore metal helmets, in addition to large metal sheets over their chests and backs. [5]Native Canadians of the West Coast wore both carved wooden helmets and chest armor made from wood and leather. [6]Nature protects the turtle and the armadillo with permanent armor. [7]Even with body armor largely absent from the modern soldier's uniform, the helmet still remains as a reminder of the vulnerability of the human body.

2. _____ _____

3. [1]I'd much rather read a book than see a movie. [2]When you read, you can imagine for yourself what characters look like and how they sound. [3]You can pick up a book at any time and not have to line up for a film to begin. [4]It is true, however, that you can do the same with videos. [5]A book goes with you to be read anywhere—you never have to be in a specific place. [6]When you find a passage you like, you can reread it or just pause and think about things. [7]Of course, it's always fun to be in a theater with other people.

3. _____ _____

_____

4. [1]During the last quarter of the twentieth century, the lives of Western women reflected dramatic social changes. [2]Women were more educated than ever before. [3]Many institutions were criticized for not recruiting more women to major in science and mathematics. [4]Access to institutions of higher learning and professional schools allowed women to participate in the work force in the areas of education, law, medicine, and business throughout the world, whether it was in Canada, the United States, or the Soviet Union. [5]Women had been active in the politics of the liberation of peoples in the 1960s. [6]These activities served to heighten women's collective awareness of the disparities between their own situations and the role of men in Western societies: women worked at home without pay; in the workplace, women received less than men for the same work.

4. _____ _____

_____

82. BEYOND THE SENTENCE: PARAGRAPH COHERENCE—TRANSITIONS

(Study Section 91, Effective Paragraphs.)

For each item, choose from the list the **transitional expression** that fits most logically in the space. Then write the number of that expression (**1** to **10**) in the blank at the right.
(For some items there is more than one possible answer.)

1.	**Afterward**	5.	**However**	8.	**On the other hand**
2.	**Consequently**	6.	**Meanwhile**	9.	**That is**
3.	**Even so**	7.	**Nevertheless**	10.	**Therefore**
4.	**Formerly**				

Example: I think. _____, I am.   10
                                                                                  _____

1. The night of the ball, we danced every step we knew. _____, we strolled on the moonlit beach.

   1. _____

2. There is widespread agreement that women can do any job. _____, women graduates may still find the job market unresponsive in some professional fields.

   2. _____

3. The computer has become the tool of choice for writers. _____, despite software that is easy to use, some writers still refuse to give up their typewriters.

   3. _____

4. Divorce may have a negative effect on children. _____, children of divorce—especially women—are more likely to divorce than children of intact families.

   4. _____

5. Canadians seem to enjoy watching in-depth discussions about major news events; _____, people who are experts are often approached by television networks.

   5. _____

6. A person speaking to members of his or her own family uses language that is informal and intimate. A person speaking to a large group, _____, is likely to choose different words and a different tone of voice.

   6. _____

7. If you toss a coin repeatedly and it comes up heads each time, common sense tells you to expect tails to turn up soon. _____, the chances of heads coming up remain the same for each toss of the coin.

   7. _____

8. Today, computers are inexpensive enough that most offices and schools can afford them. _____, the cost of these machines was prohibitive.

   8. _____

9. In general, a small animal acclimatizes better than a large one. _____, the small animal finds it easier to adjust to changes in the environment.

   9. _____

10. It was evident to the leader and to the other jurors that they were hopelessly deadlocked. _____, the leader sent word to the judge that they were unable to agree on a verdict.

   10. _____

83. BEYOND THE SENTENCE: BIBLIOGRAPHIC FORM

(Open-Book Exercise—Study Section 93, The Reference List.)

Write **1** if entire entry is **correct** in form.
Write **0** if the entry contains any error in form (including punctuation). Circle the error.
For Part I of this exercise, use the **MLA** style.

1. Book	Bamberger, Jeanne S., and Howard Brofsky. <u>The Art of Listening: Developing Musical Perception,</u> 2nd ed. New York: Harper, 1972.	1. _____
2. Book	Blanche Ellsworth, and Arnold Keller. <u>English Simplified.</u> Third Canadian ed. Toronto: HarperCollins, 1996.	2. _____
3. Book	Horvath, Polly. <u>The Happy Yellow Car.</u> HarperCollins, Toronto: 1994.	3. _____
4. Journal Article	Woodcock, George. <u>Empires Of Blood And Sun</u>. "Canadian Literature" 142 (Fall/Winter 1994): 50—64.	4. _____
5. Newspaper Article	McGran, Kevin. "Gretzky Tour Closes On Road." <u>Victoria Times–Colonist</u> Dec. 15, 1994: C22.	5. _____
6. Encyclopedia Article	*German Volga Republic.* "The New Columbia Encyclopedia." 1975 ed.	6. _____
7. Magazine Article	Stringer, Dick. "No More Clearcuts!" Eco–Defense 9 August 1994: 5.	7. _____
8. Magazine Article	Pape, Jake. "Inside the Sacred Hopi Homeland." *National Geographic* (162 1982: 607–629).	8. _____
9. Article in a Collection	Crofton, Mark; "Canadians: A Coat of Many Shades." <u>The Old Consensus.</u> Ed. Helen Rogers Greene. Vancouver: Partisan Press, 1994, 140–156.	9. _____
10. Journal Article	Simpson, Michele L. and Sherrie L. Nist. "Textbook Annotation: An Effective and Efficient Study Strategy for College Students." <u>Journal of Reading</u> 34 (1990): 122–129.	10. _____

Write **1** if entire entry is **correct** in form.
Write **0** if the entry contains any error in form (including punctuation).
Circle the error.
For Part II of this exercise, use the **APA** style.

1. Book	Covey, S R. (1989). <u>The 7 habits of highly effective people</u> New York: Simon & Schuster.	1. _____
2. Book	Baker, M (Ed.). (1994). <u>Canada's changing families : challenges to public policy</u>. Ottawa: Vanier Institute of the Family.	2. _____
3. Newspaper Article	Northrup, M (1994, December 6). Strike date looms for mills. "The Province," p. 1C	3. _____
4. Book	Berton P. (1994). Winter Toronto: Stoddart.	4. _____
5. Book	Martin, D. (1991, 2nd ed.). <u>How to be a successful student</u>. San Anselmo, California: Martin Press.	5. _____
6. Book	Batten, J. <u>The leafs.</u> Toronto: Key Porter. 1994.	6. _____

7. **Magazine Article**	Edwards, P. (1994, November 4): <u>The last picture show</u>. Out West, pp. 36–39.	7. _____
8. **Article in Collection, Editor**	Wieder, D. L. & Pratt, S. (1990). "On being a recognizable Indian among Indians." In D. Carbaugh (Ed.), <u>Cultural communication and intercultural contact.</u> Hillsdale, New Jersey: Lawrence Erlbaum Associates, Publishers.	8. _____
9. **Book**	C. McCall & Clarkson, S. (1994). <u>Trudeau and Our times</u>. Volume 2: The heroic delusion. Toronto: McClelland & Stewart.	9. _____
10. **Book, Editor**	Rabil, A. (Ed.). (1988). <u>Renaissance humanism.</u> Philadelphia: University of Pennsylvania Press.	10. _____

84. DOCUMENTATION

(Open-Book Exercise—Study Section 92, Citations, and Section 94, Endnotes and Footnotes.)

Write **1** for each item that is **correct** in form.
Write **0** for each that is **incorrect,** and circle the error.

Part I: MLA style

1. Text   Farb states that language is needed to make sense of life's experiences.[1]

1. _____

2. Footnote   [1]Peter Farb, <u>Word Play: What Happens When People Talk</u> (New York: Random House, 1973).

2. _____

3. Text   According to Termin, who studied intellectually gifted children, "success, if not intelligence, ran in families."[2]

3. _____

4. Footnote   [2]Greene, Peter R., <u>The Peacekeeper: Canada's As Policeman</u> (Halifax: Option Press, 1992) 182.

4. _____

5. Text   White observes that while women comprise over three-fourths of most general banking staffs, less than ten percent hold managerial positions.[4]

5. _____

6. Footnote   [4]Jane White, <u>A Few Good Women: Breaking Barriers to the Top Management,</u> (Englewood Cliffs, New Jersey: Prentice Hall). 150.

6. _____

7. Text   Cohen and Parker observe that romanticism has never disappeared, although it has changed it voice many times. "10"

7. _____

8. Footnote   [10]Seth Cohen, and Elizabeth Parker, <u>What Was Romanticism.</u> (Montreal: McGill–Queen's University Press, 1992).

8. _____

9. Text   (The paper cites two works by the same author.)
Hennings offers strategies for helping students become more proficient readers in their history courses.[17]Hennings

9. _____

10. Footnote   (This writer and work have been cited earlier in this paper.)
[17]Hennings, On Knowing.

10. _____

85. ACHIEVEMENT TEST: GRAMMAR

Sentences

Write **1** if the boldface expression is **one complete sentence**.
Write **2** if it is a **fragment**.
Write **3** if it is a **comma splice** or **fused sentence** (run-on).

Example: Having completely slipped its moorings.   2
_____

1. He decided not to go. *After buying the tickets and packing his bags.*   1. _____

2. I was urged to do two things. *To drop out of college and to go to work.*   2. _____

3. *He will attend college, his high-school grades are good enough.*   3. _____

4. In the 1980s, the price of famous paintings increased 150 percent because of investors. *Then these same investors were no longer interested in purchasing art.*   4. _____

5. *When does abstract art become just scribbles?*   5. _____

6. *An hour before the concert started.* The director became ill.   6. _____

7. *Our guests having arrived, we sat down to dinner.*   7. _____

8. The Internet will be replaced. *This computer network cannot quickly transmit books or full-motion video, the newest network can.*   8. _____

9. *The storm having washed out the bridge.* We had to spend the night in town.   9. _____

10. Sir Thisby invited me to play cricket. *A game I had never even watched.*   10. _____

11. *The high humidity forced us to move the picnic inside, it was just too hot to eat outside.*   11. _____

12. *The woman who tape-records the physics lectures.*   12. _____

13. *The snow continues to fall even though the weather forecasters predicted rain.*   13. _____

14. Allen used a week's vacation. *To sand and refinish the hardwood floors in his home.*   14. _____

15. Aaron always told his family that he wanted to be a physician, *however, he secretly dreamed of running off to New York to study acting.*   15. _____

Grammar

Write **1** if the boldface expression is used correctly.
Write **0** if it is used incorrectly.

Example: There **was** laughing, singing, and shouting coming from the dorm.   0
_____

1. The dean said *that* if she could help us *that* she would be glad to see us.   1. _____

2. During the summer she trained horses, *which* assisted her financially.   2. _____

3. In this mall *are* a child-care facility, an adult literacy school, and a large discount store.   3. _____

4. Cousin Max, along with his twin daughters and their cats, *were* waiting at my front door.   4. _____

5. The conductor asked each of the musicians to mark *their* score.   5. _____

6. A copy of *Chatelaine* and a copy of *Rolling Stone* **was** in Dr. Moore's waiting room.   6. _____

7. The taxi driver gave Tony and *I* a scornful glance.   7. _____

8. The ticket agent gave Ed and *I* seats that were behind home plate.   8. _____

9. Every committee member **was** given a copy of the report.   9. _____

10. **Refusing to pay high interest,** consumers are cutting up their credit cards.   10. _____

11. Parking restrictions apply **not only** to students **but also** to visitors.   11. _____

12. His mother wanted him to become a corporation lawyer. **This** kept Leonard in college.   12. _____

13. He tried to **promptly and efficiently** complete each task assigned to him.   13. _____

14. All of **we** students protested the new attendance regulation.   14. _____

15. **Having more than an hour to kill,** there was time to stroll through the village.   15. _____

16. His plans included **landing a well-paying internship and to spend as much time as possible with his girlfriend.**   16. _____

17. **Being 265 years old,** it seemed a sacrilege to cut down the giant pine.   17. _____

18. I like **swimming and to relax** in the warm sunshine.   18. _____

19. We wondered why the list of courses **was** not posted yet.   19. _____

20. There are few people I respect as much as **her**.   20. _____

21. **Is** either of the two bands ready to go on?   21. _____

22. **Who** did you see at the game last night?   22. _____

23. Everyone who plays the 6/49 hopes that **their** ticket will win the million-dollar jackpot.   23. _____

24. The secretary behaved **differently** once he was fired.   24. _____

25. Aggression **is when** one nation attacks another without provocation.   25. _____

26. Financial aid will be made available to **whoever** shows a need for it.   26. _____

27. My reason for working last summer was **that** I wanted to buy a car.   27. _____

28. He coached soccer and joined two service clubs. **It** was expected of him by his associates.   28. _____

29. Fritz and **myself** followed the tall, mysterious stranger.   29. _____

30. **Who** do you think will be candidates for the office of student-body president?   30. _____

31. Neither Joan nor her two attendants **was** asked to appear on television.   31. _____

32. There **was** at least eight persons involved in the traffic accident.   32. _____

33. Between you and *I*, Martin has only a slim chance of promotion this year.   33. _____

34. **Is** there any objections to your opening a pub in the neighbourhood?   34. _____

35. She is one of six applicants who **are** to be interviewed tomorrow.   35. _____

36. Are you sure that it was **they** whom you saw in the post office?   36. _____

37. My adviser suggested that I take Japanese. **That** was fine with me.   37. _____

38. Jane is the **friendliest** of the two sisters.   38. _____

39. You will never find anyone more responsible than **her**.   39. _____

40. Paul cooks **like he was** a professional chef.   40. _____

41. Each of the players **has** two passes for all home games.   41. _____

42. Why not give the keys to **whomever** you think will be in charge?   42. _____

43. Did the committee approve of *his* assuming the chair? 43. _____

44. Several of *we* students had decided to start a petition addressed to the deans. 44. _____

45. In the package *were* a book, a shirt, and a video. 45. _____

46. The coach, as well as the manager and the players, *was* sure of winning. 46. _____

47. *Knowing of his parents' disapproval*, it seemed wise for him to reconsider his plan to drop out of school. 47. _____

48. He had decided to *only* spend two dollars for a gift. 48. _____

49. If he *were* more tactful, he would have fewer enemies. 49. _____

50. Fiona chose Dominic and *I* to be her audience. 50. _____

51. Neither the camp director nor the hikers *was* aware of their danger. 51. _____

52. He purchased the only one of the books that *was* of any value to him. 52. _____

53. The doctor's report suggested that my wife and *I* consider adoption. 53. _____

54. He told Steve and *I* to try to sell tickets at the dance. 54. _____

55. My friends and *myself* enjoyed our skiing trip. 55. _____

56. Each of the students *plans* to attend the career fair. 56. _____

57. The poor writing and the sloppiness of your research *forces* me to fail this essay. 57. _____

58. *Shouting loudly*, Josh's noise was unbearable. 58. _____

59. I hate rewriting my papers even though it helps *you* earn a better grade. 59. _____

60. When the Flames and the Canucks play, I know *they* will win. 60. _____

86. ACHIEVEMENT TEST: PUNCTUATION

Write **1** if the punctuation in brackets is **correct.**
Write **0** if it is **incorrect.**
(Use only one number in each blank.)

Example: Stuart took lessons in using[,] word
processing.   0

1. Maple Ridge, British Columbia[,] was their
last stop on the trip west.   1. _____

2. The neighbours[,] who own the
barking dog[,] refuse to do anything
about their noisy pet.   2. _____

3. I wanted to call on the Blanks, but I
wasn't sure which house was their[']s.   3. _____

4. Our flight having been announced[,] we
hurried to board our plane.   4. _____

5. We went for a ride in the country[.]
The day being warm and balmy.   5. _____

6. When Julie returned the book, it['s]
cover was torn.   6. _____

7. Haven't you often heard it said, "Haste
makes waste["?]   7. _____

8. "Wouldn't you like to go to the party
with us?"[,] asked the girl across the
hall.   8. _____

9. He said, "Let's walk across the
campus.["]["]It's such a beautiful
evening."   9. _____

10. Enrollment is up to three[-]thousand
students this semester.   10. _____

11. Twenty[-]six students have
volunteered to serve on various
committees.   11. _____

12. Dear Sir[;] I believe that I am just the
person who can run your business
more efficiently.   12. _____

13. After you have finished your sociology
assignment[,] shall we go to the
nightclub?   13. _____

14. Billy Budd struck Claggart[,] because
he could not express himself any other
way.   14. _____

15. Fuchsia is the colour you ordered[,]
isn't it?   15. _____

16. We were early[;] as a matter of fact,
we were the first of the guests to arrive. 16. _____

17. "If you are really serious about your
work," the instructor said[,] "you'll
succeed."   17. _____

18. Johnson had little praise for the
current government[;] calling it a
collection of tired liars.   18. _____

19. The band recorded its first album in
the spring[,] and followed it with a
concert tour in the summer.   19. _____

20. She had hoped to arrange a two
month[']s tour of Korea and Japan.   20. _____

21. This is your office[,] Ms. Foster; I trust
that it will be satisfactory.   21. _____

22. The next stockholders' meeting is
scheduled for August 9, 1996[,] but
will be open to only major investors.   22. _____

23. All the drivers[,] who were not
wearing seatbelts[,] were being
stopped by the police.   23. _____

24. Because she had watched television
until after midnight[;] she overslept.   24. _____

25. A medal was awarded to Jane Cox,
an engineering student[,] for rescuing
the children.   25. _____

26. Professor Thomas was asked to
create a course for the womens[']
studies department.   26. _____

27. The little boy in the centre of the
photograph[,] would later own his
own company.   27. _____

28. "As for who has written the winning
essay[—]well, I haven't as yet heard
from the judges," said Mr. Hawkins.   28. _____

29. What he described about the massive oil spill in Alaska[,] filled us with horror. 29. _____

30. I asked Elizabeth what we should do about plane reservations[?]. 30. _____

31. The newly elected officers are Cleon Jones, president[;] Ray Ng, vice-president[;] and Terry Pascale, secretary-treasurer. 31. _____

32. Many weeks before school was over[;] she was planning a vacation. 32. _____

33. We followed the trail over several ridges[,] and along the edge of two mountain lakes. 33. _____

34. Before going to Europe, I had many matters to attend to[;] such as making reservations, buying clothes, and getting a passport. 34. _____

35. Having a good sense of humour helps you put things in perspective[;] certainly, it's better than brooding. 35. _____

36. The ticket agent inquired ["]if we were planning to stop in Paris.["]. 36. _____

37. The television networks have aired seven different reality-based police shows that portray police in their squad-car patrols[,] and in their station-house interactions. 37. _____

38. Marcia learned that all foods[,] which are high in calories[,] were to be avoided. 38. _____

39. We were told to read ["]Ode to a Nightingale,["] a poem by Keats. 39. _____

40. The alumni magazine had a column cleverly entitled ["]Grad-Tidings.["] 40. _____

41. A trail construction team could provide[:] education, training, and work for dozens of unemployed teenagers. 41. _____

42. Some people wish to change some words in ["]O Canada["] to remove the repetitions. 42. _____

43. She hurried toward us[,] her books clasped under her arm[,] to tell us the good news. 43. _____

44. The audience wanted him to sing one more song[;] however, he refused. 44. _____

45. The enthusiastic response of his audience[;] however, made him change his mind. 45. _____

46. She found a note in her mailbox: "Sorry to have missed you. The Lawson[']s." 46. _____

47. His father wanted him to major in engineering[;] he wanted to major in music. 47. _____

48. Chris decided that he wanted a quiet vacation[,] not one full of schedules and guided tours. 48. _____

49. He had gone to the library[. B]ecause he needed more material for his term paper. 49. _____

50. Her program included courses in English[,] social science[,] and chemistry. 50. _____

51. The two women, not having very much in common[;] found very little to say to each other. 51. _____

52. To be able to speak confidently before a group[;] Donna enrolled in a speech class. 52. _____

53. Ms. Whitney, who is the gym teacher, came to the dance[;] with Mr. Martin, who is the football coach. 53. _____

54. When Hurricane Andrew hit the southern tip of Florida[,] it caused over $20 billion in damage. 54. _____

55. "Some of the members wer[']ent able to pay their dues," she said. 55. _____

56. Frank Anderson[,] who is on the debating team[,] is an excellent speaker. 56. _____

57. "All motorists[,] who fail to stop at a crosswalk[,] should be put in jail!" said one parent. 57. _____

58. Looking at me sweetly, Mark replied, "No[,] there is no way in the world I'd ever marry you." 58. _____

59. George enrolled in a course in home economics; Lise[,] in a course in woodworking. 59. _____

60. "Haven't I met you somewhere before?"[,] he asked. 60. _____

61. "It's most unlikely["!] she said, turning away. 61. _____

62. Joe Ackerman, a man[,] whom I had met in college, called to see me. 62. _____

63. New commuter train systems are inexpensive to develop[,] where tracks are already in place. 63. _____

64. He moved to Edmonton[,] where he attended university. 64. _____

65. We were[,] on the other hand[,] not surprised at his decision. 65. _____

66. Using modern video cameras[,] the graduate student conducted a high-tech search for Scotland's Loch Ness monster. 66. _____

67. Listen to the arguments of both speakers[,] then decide which side you favour. 67. _____

68. At the beginning of the dinner party[;] I discovered that the main course was undercooked. 68. _____

69. Our dog Sam always greets us at the door[,] and barks until we pay attention to him. 69. _____

70. Irma Williamson[,] who teaches mathematics at the University of Toronto[,] will lead the panel discussion. 70. _____

71. The conference sponsored by our fraternity was successful[,] especially the sessions concerning community-service projects. 71. _____

72. The music created[,] a more relaxed atmosphere. 72. _____

73. Jack displayed a unique[?] talent when he created a painting with spaghetti sauce, yellow mustard, and pickles. 73. _____

74. The children[,] on the other hand[,] were content to wear last year's coats and boots. 74. _____

75. The teenager used the word [*like*] throughout her conversation. 75. _____

87. ACHIEVEMENT TEST: MECHANICS, SPELLING, USAGE

Capitalization

Write **1** if the boldface word(s) **follow** the rules of capitalization.
Write **0** if they **do not.**

Example: Uncle Spike is their *Shortstop.*	0
Example: Their shortstop is *Uncle Spike.*	1
1. I barely passed *french.*	1. ————
2. My brother attends *High School.*	2. ————
3. She is *President* of her class.	3. ————
4. I belong to the *Science Club.*	4. ————
5. He plays for Queen's *University.*	5. ————
6. We cheered the *canadian* flag.	6. ————
7. My *Uncle* plays hockey.	7. ————
8. I told *Grandfather* that he was being very kind to me.	8. ————
9. He likes living in the *West.*	9. ————
10. I shall go east next *Spring.*	10. ————
11. She enrolled in *History 101.*	11. ————
12. I visited an *Indian* village near Bombay.	12. ————
13. Anna attends a *University.*	13. ————
14. He enjoys his *history* course.	14. ————
15. Fetch; *Sit.*	15. ————
16. "You are," *he* said, "the one."	16. ————
17. "What," he asked, "*is* wrong?"	17. ————
18. We met on *New Year's Eve.*	18. ————
19. The note began, "My *Dear* John."	19. ————
20. I'm going to be a *Star.*	20. ————

Abbreviations and Numbers

Write 1 **if the boldface abbreviation or number is used** correctly.
Write 0 **if it is used** incorrectly.

Example: *2's* company, three's a crowd.	0
1. This is her *20th* birthday.	1. ————
2. Thank God it's *Fri.*	2. ————

3. My dog Spot is *3*.   3. _____

4. I saw him on Government *St.* today.   4. _____

5. Emmy was born on July *5th,* 1987.   5. _____

6. Please meet me at *10 o'clock.*   6. _____

7. He released *two hundred* red balloons at the dance.   7. _____

8. The train leaves at *8* p.m.   8. _____

9. Dinner was served at *six o'clock.*   9. _____

10. Tara Blank, *Ph.D.,* spoke first.   10. _____

11. Lunch cost *12* dollars.   11. _____

12. *Ms.* Horvath, take a letter.   12. _____

13. Harry Brown's monthly salary is now *$1,299.53.*   13. _____

14. The Fox *Co.* is selling out.   14. _____

15. We learned that *14* students received scholarship awards.   15. _____

Spelling

In each sentence, **one** boldface word is **misspelled;** write its number in the blank.

Example: (1) **Their** (2) **questionnaries** have been (3) **received.**   _____2_____

1. (1) *It's* (2) *unusual* for him to be so (3) *conscientous,* isn't it?   1. _____

2. The open (1) *cemetery* gates permitted an (2) *excellent* (3) *opportunity* for Karloff's laboratory
   assistant.   2. _____

3. Does the (1) *psychology* (2) *proffesor* require (3) *written* reports?   3. _____

4. I (1) *beleive* that he is (2) *benefiting* from (3) *competition* with the athletes.   4. _____

5. The (1) *first-year* student learned that a (2) *knowledge* of (3) *grammer* is helpful. 5. _____

6. A (1) *fourth* such disaster threatens the very (2) *existance* of the Yukon (3) *environment.* 6. _____

7. He considers that it's (1) *definately* a (2) *privilege* to work in this (3) *article.* 7. _____

8. The (1) *principal* (2) *complimented* her for her (3) *excellant* performance.   8. _____

9. It was (1) *apparent* that she had (2) *profitted* by listening to his (3) *advice.*   9. _____

10. We (1) *imediately* became (2) *familiar* with the requirements for a (3) *license.*   10. _____

11. Is it (1) *permissable* to ask him to (2) *recommend* me for a (3) *government* position? 11. _____

12. He showed a (1) *tendency* to (2) *reminisce* about his early (3) *achievments.*   12. _____

13. The test pilot felt enormous (1) *optimism* after her third (2) *repitition* of the dangerous
    (3) *maneuver.*   13. _____

14. It's (1) *concievable* that the (2) *omission* might prove (3) *disastrous.*   14. _____

15. She was not (1) *conscious* of being (2) *unnecessarily* (3) *persistant* about the matter. 15. _____

Usage

Write **1** if the boldface expression is used **correctly.**
Write **0** if it is used **incorrectly.**

Example: *In actual fact,* Karen was there.   _0_

1. I was not *altogether* amused.   1. _____
2. Rover looks *sort* of sick.   2. _____
3. They are all old; for *instants,* Grayson is eighty-six.   3. _____
4. Billy cried when his balloon *burst.*   4. _____
5. Try to make *fewer* mistakes.   5. _____
6. He earned no interest on his *principal.*   6. _____
7. *Can* I add your name to the list?   7. _____
8. The judge would hear no *farther* arguments.   8. _____
9. I'm in real trouble, *aren't I?*   9. _____
10. The team was *plenty* angry.   10. _____
11. The parent *persuaded* her child to take out the garbage.   11. _____
12. He notified *most* of his creditors.   12. _____
13. She has *less* excuses than I.   13. _____
14. Saul made an *illusion* to *Hamlet.*   14. _____
15. Was the murderer *hanged?*   15. _____
16. Eleanor feels *some* better now.   16. _____
17. Her ideas were different *from* mine.   17. _____
18. I had *already* signed the check.   18. _____
19. Jay sounds *like* he's serious this time.   19. _____
20. I dislike *those kind* of promises.   20. _____
21. He became *real* independent.   21. _____
22. The cat is *lying* by the fire.   22. _____
23. She *generally always* works hard.   23. _____
24. He does *good* in math courses.   24. _____
25. His speech *implied* that he would raise taxes.   25. _____

88. ACHIEVEMENT TEST: DOCUMENTATION

(Open-Book Exercise—Study Sections 92–94, Documentation.)

Write **1** for each bibliographic entry that is **correct** in form.
Write **0** for each that is **incorrect,** and circle the error.

Part I: MLA Style

1. **Book**   Hunter, Douglas. <u>Open ice</u>; the Tim Horton story. Toronto: Viking, 1994.   1. _____

2. **Journal Article**   Mallon, Jeffrey V. "Reading Science." Journal of Reading 34 (1991):
                            324–338.   2. _____

3. **Newspaper Article**   Vincent, Valerie. <u>No Agreement in Sight for Budget Cuts.</u> "Calgary
                            Herald" 3 March 1994: 1.   3. _____

Part II: APA Style

4. **Book**   Nash, K. (1994). <u>The microphone wars: a history of triumph and
                            betrayal at the CBC</u>. Toronto: McClelland & Stewart.   4. _____

5. **Magazine Article**   Carson, L. (1994, October 11). "The theory behind theory"
                            Maclean's p. 61.   5. _____

6. **Journal Article**   Thistlewaite, L. L. (1990). "Critical reading for at-risk students.
                            <u>Journal of Reading,</u> (33), pp. 586–593.   6. _____

Write **1** for each citation that is **correct** in form.
Write **0** for each that is incorrect.

Part III: MLA Style

7. **Direct Quote**   According to a recent study of college students, "23 percent spent
                            no time at all on required reading during their entire college
                            career." (Douglas 175)   7. _____

8. **Paraphrase**   Douglas observes that many of the new student activities on
                            campus are not closely related to intellectual pursuits (172).   8. _____

Part IV: APA Style

9. Paraphrase Osborne (1989) reports that competent children have parents who encourage their children to play independently. 9. _____

10. Direct Quote Osborne (1989) observes that the majority of television programs contain violence; in fact, studies reveal that there are "five violent acts per hour during prime time" (page 83). 10. _____

A List of Grammatical Terms

The following chart gives brief definitions, examples, and nonexamples of the grammatical terms you'll read about most often in these exercises. Refer to *English Simplified* for more information.

<u>Term</u>	<u>What It *Is* or *Does*</u>	<u>Examples</u>	<u>Nonexamples</u>
Adjective	Describes a noun	a *fast* runner (describes the noun *runner*)	He runs *fast* (describes the verb runs)
Appositive	A noun that renames another	Polly Horvath, **the writer,** lives in Victoria. (The appositive follows the writer's name.)	*Polly Horvath,* the writer, lives in Victoria.
Adverb	Describes a verb, adjective, or another adverb	He runs *fast* (describes the verb *run*) He runs *very* fast (describes the adverb *fast*) He is an *extremely* fast runner (describes the adjective *fast*)	He is a *fast* runner. (Here, *fast* is an adjective.)
Clause	A group of words with a subject and a predicate. A *main clause* can stand by itself and make complete sense; a *dependent clause* must be attached to a main clause.	*He is a fast runner.* (A main clause) *if he is a fast runner* (A dependent clause that must be attached to some main clause; for example, *He would win.*)	a *fast runner* (merely a noun and its adjective)
Complement	Completes the meaning of the verb.	<u>Direct Object:</u> Becca threw the *ball.* (Says what got thrown.) <u>Indirect Object:</u> She threw the ball to *me.* (Says who benefited by the ball being thrown.) <u>Subjective Complement:</u> She is a *pitcher.* (Renames the subject *she* after the linking verb *is.*) <u>Objective Complement:</u> The team named Alou *manager.* (Follows the direct object *Alou* and renames it.)	*Becca* threw the ball. (Says who did the action rather than received it.)
Conjunction	A word that joins.	<u>Coordinating conjunction:</u> Joins things of equal importance: Men *and* women. Poor *but* honest. <u>Subordinating Conjunction:</u> Joins a dependent clause to a main clause: I left *when* she arrived	I left *at* noon. (*At* is a preposition.)

Term	What It *Is* or *Does*	Examples	Nonexamples
Fragment	Word that cannot stand by itself and make complete sense.	*when I saw them* (a dependent clause) *from British Columbia* (a prepositional phrase)	*They went from British Columbia to Newfoundland.* (A main clause that can stand by itself)
Noun	Names a person, place, animal, or thing.	*Tom Ottawa cat book*	*throw* (a verb) *red* (an adjective)
Phrase	A group of words without a subject and a verb.	*from Newfoundland* (a prepositional phrase) *to see the king* (an infinitive phrase) *built of bricks* (a participial phrase) *building houses* (a gerund phrase)	*He is from Newfoundland.* (a main clause)
Predicate	The part of the sentence that speaks about the subject.	The man *threw the ball.* (says what the subject did)	The *man* threw the ball. (The man performed the action.)
Pronoun	A word that replaces a noun.	*He* will be here soon. (*He* takes the place of the man's name.)	*Jonathan* will be here soon. (*Jonathan* is a noun.)
Subject	The person or thing about whom the sentence speaks.	*Polly* writes children's books.	Polly *writes children's books.* (Writes children's books is the predicate, that is, the action she performs.)
Verb	Says what the subject either does or is	She *buys* seashells. She *is* smart.	*Rebecca* is smart. (*Rebecca* is a noun.)

166

DIAGRAMING

Diagraming is a method of analyzing sentences and of visually depicting parts of speech and their functions in sentences. Though diagrams can grow complex, their basic principle is simple: Everything in the complete subject is written to the left of the main vertical line; everything in the complete predicate, to the right. All the main parts of a sentence are written on or above the main horizontal line; all the secondary parts, below the main horizontal line.

Simple sentence

An old friend from school often sends me very funny postcards.

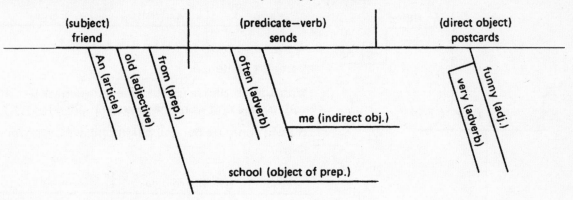

Simple sentence with compound parts

Romeo and Juliet fell in love and planned a secret wedding.

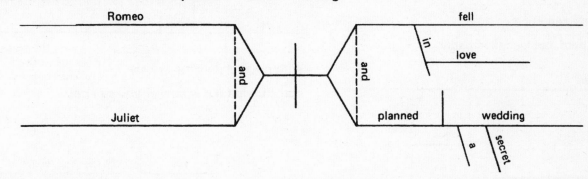

Verbals and verbal phrases

Used as modifiers

Reeling under our attacks (participial phrase), the *decimated* (participle) enemy requested a truce *to arrange a surrender* (infinitive phrase).

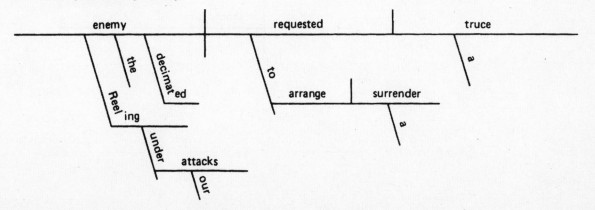

Verbals and verbal phrases

Used as nouns

They denied *having tried to embezzle funds by falsifying data.* (Italicized words are a gerund phrase: within that phrase are an infinitive phrase, *to embezzle funds,* and another gerund phrase, *falsifying data.*)

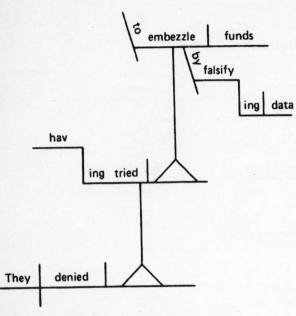

Compound sentence

We tried hard, but we failed badly.

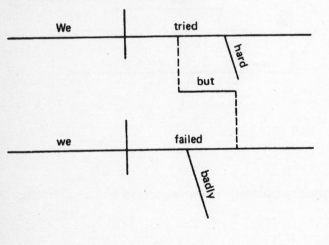

Complex sentence

With adjective clause (dotted line between relative pronoun and antecedent)

I respect a person *who can resist pressure.*

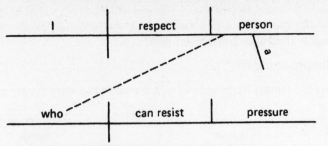

Complex sentence

With adverb clause (dotted line between verb of adverb clause and word the clause modifies)

We will continue our campaign *until we make Jones mayor.*

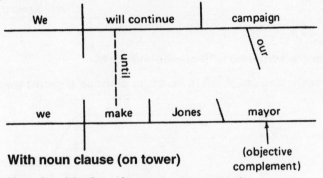

(objective complement)

With noun clause (on tower)

You should take *whatever you can get.*

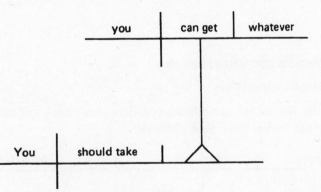

That you will succeed is almost certain.

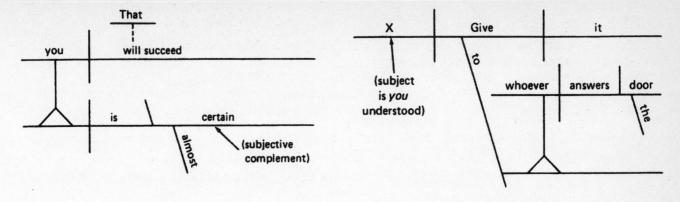

Give it to whoever answers the door.